The Scottish 1

A play

Graham Holliday

Samuel French – London
New York – Sydney – Toronto – Hollywood

Please see page 61 for further copyright information

CHARACTERS

Michael
Lynne, his wife
Frank
Alan
Barnaby
Eric   } members of the Shellsfoot Thespians
Geraldine
Sally
Fiona
Mary
Daisy
Les Dye, an estate agent
Jackie, a receptionist

The action of the play takes place in various locations

Time: the present

The Scottish Play

The original version of *The Scottish Play* was a 55-minute radio play, broadcast on BBC Radio Four, on 19th September, 1985, with the following cast:

Michael	Geoffrey Collins
Lynne	Carole Nimmons
Frank	Edward de Souza
Alan	Graham Chinn
Barnaby	Robin Summers
Geraldine	Mary Wimbush
Jackie	Jenny Funnell
Les Dye	David Sinclair
Porter	Peter Acre
1st Witch	Tessa Worsley

Directed by **John Cardy**

It was subsequently performed as a rehearsed reading by members of the Royal Shakespeare Company at the Almeida Theatre, London, on 19th July, 1986. The cast included Ian Talbot as Michael and Janet Dale as Lynne

TO JILLIE

SETTING

The various locations should be distinguished by the use of lighting, different areas of the stage, and a few pieces of furniture. The places depicted are: various parts of the church hall (the stage during a performance of a country-house thriller, the dressing-room, the stage during auditions and rehearsals, and the auditorium during a jumble sale); the offices of Cooper & Dye; Michael's and Lynne's lounge and dining-room; a table in a pub; and Shellsfoot Town Hall (the stage, the women's dressing-room, and the lighting box). In addition, some sections take place inside Michael's mind, and we should see his face lit and the figures in his imagination moving in shadow.

ACT I

*The play begins in Michael's mind, in black-out and silence. Michael is
standing at one side of the stage, and Sally, Fiona and Mary—as the three
witches in "Macbeth" Act One Scene One—form a tableau at the other.
Three long gusts of wind, each growing in volume to a peak then subsiding.
Then a quieter and continuous sound of wind, which lasts until the witches' exit*

Michael Thunder.

A roll of thunder

Lightning.

*A flash of lightning, too brief for us to see anything distinctly, and an
immediate crash of thunder. Michael's face is now lit by a gradually
brightening spot*

Enter . . . three . . . witches . . .

The witches are now seen, in murky light

Sally When shall we three meet again,
In thunder, lightning, or in rain?
Fiona When the hurlyburly's done,
When the battle's lost and won.
Mary That will be ere the set of sun.

They freeze

Michael All three of them should be clothed in black, and seen against a
backcloth of black velvet. Three witches, matching figures, but each a
distinct character. The first . . . (*he thinks it out*) . . . domineering, with a
strident, piercing voice.
Sally Where the place?

They freeze

Michael The second, a warped humourist, delighting in the evil of her
spells.
Fiona Upon the heath!

They freeze

Michael Number three, now, what for her? . . . secretive, yes, dark and
muttering. The most dangerous of them all.
Mary There to meet with——
Michael (*the idea suddenly occurring to him*) All three together!

Sally
Fiona } (*together*) Macbeth!
Mary

Thunder

Michael Now ... the cries of wild beasts, and shrieking spirits ...

We hear cries and shrieks as he says it

Sally   I come, Graymalkin!
Fiona   Paddock calls!
Mary   Anon ...

The witches move closer together

Michael (*intense*) They draw together like three drops of water, losing their identities as they merge. Three into one, they link hands——

Sally
Fiona } (*together*) Fair is foul and foul is fair——
Mary

Michael Turn their backs on the audience——

Sally
Fiona } (*together*) Hover through the fog and filthy air!
Mary

Michael And ... vanish!

The light on the witches goes out, the wind grows in volume, and they leave, laughing in the darkness

Black against black, they melt into the night, and take possession of it. The world is charged with evil; all things are under its control. And the play begins.

The wind reaches a climax, then cuts off. The lights go up suddenly on the stage of the church hall, during a performance of "A Bullet in the Back" by the Shellsfoot Thespians

Michael is part of it, a young man in an ill-fitting dinner-jacket. But he is obviously paying no attention to what is going on around him. Also on the stage are Geraldine, expensively dressed and made up to look much younger than she is, Frank as a plain-clothes detective, and Eric as a respectable-looking middle-aged man

Geraldine Don't be ridiculous, Inspector. I wasn't anywhere near the place. I was out walking ... with Howard. Wasn't I, Howard?

She looks at Michael, who does not respond. Geraldine looks into the wings, sniffs with contempt at the prompter's absence, and repeats her line a little louder

Don't be ridiculous, Inspector. I wasn't anywhere near the place. I was out walking ... with Howard. Wasn't I, Howard?

Still no response from Michael

Frank (*improvising pretty well*) I'm sure Mr Garningham will . . . will corroborate your story, Lady . . . Lady Penfold . . .

Geraldine, oblivious of Frank, insistent that Michael gives her his line, goes over to him and directs the cue loudly into his ear

Geraldine Don't be ridiculous, Inspector. I wasn't anywhere near the place. I was out walking . . . with Howard. Wasn't I, Howard?

Michael (*snapping to*) Of . . . of course you were. Lady Penfold was with me, Inspector. In the woods.

Frank In the woods, eh? Well, we should be able to check that.

Geraldine (*flinching violently*) Oh . . . should you? How?

Frank Don't you remember? Constable Parry was walking through the woods when he heard the shot fired. (*He smiles*) No doubt you met him there, Lady Penfold.

They freeze, Geraldine gaping at him. The sound of a curtain coming across, and applause

Alan comes in and starts moving the furniture around

Frank goes off

Michael is about to follow him

Geraldine (*as soon as the curtain is closed, hissing loudly*) How dare you! You ruined my scene!

Alan Demarcation, boss, that's *her* job.

Michael Oh . . . sorry, Geraldine . . . I was miles away . . .

Geraldine You'd be hounded out of the professional theatre!

Michael Yeah, yeah, sure . . .

He hurries out after Frank

Geraldine (*turning on Alan*) What are you smirking at?

Alan Just admirin' the way you 'andled it.

Geraldine One has to be prepared for anything in this world. No, not there—there. (*Pointing to a cushion on the sofa*)

Alan Where d'you mean?

Geraldine There! (*She moves it a couple of inches*)

Alan 'Mazin'! Makes all the difference, dunnit!

Geraldine Just observe me, my boy, and you'll learn a great deal about the way things are done in the drama.

They go out

The lights crossfade to Frank, changing in a cramped dressing-room

Michael comes in

Pause

Michael Don't say it.

Frank I wasn't going to.

Pause

Michael What?

Frank Mm?

Michael There's obviously something in particular that you weren't going to say.

Frank Well, since you mention it, I wasn't going to pass any remark about the complete balls-up you made of that last scene.

Michael That's very considerate of you, Frank.

Frank Under normal circumstances, I'd say it could happen to anyone, and it's not your fault. But you must admit you've hardly been the embodiment of concentrated effort these last few weeks. It's not even as if we're half-way through a two-year run—it's only the first night of three.

Michael I really appreciate the way you're avoiding the subject.

Frank Oh, what are friends for?

Michael But it's so bloody boring! It's formula stuff, bang bang, body in the library, least likely suspect and Bob's your bloody uncle. How can you dedicate yourself to a load of crap like that?

Frank One can take a certain pride in one's performance, even if the play's rubbish. One can . . . try to . . . arrange it artistically in the dustbin.

Michael Well, I can't.

Frank Look, Michael, why did you take the part? Nobody held a gun to your head.

Michael Oh, worse than guns. Moral pressure. Blackmail. Bail out the Thespians in their hour of need—I had a lead in the last two shows—duty to the Group—Henry was desperate for a man——

Frank
Michael } (*together*) As usual——

Michael And I couldn't think of an excuse fast enough. That's my trouble, I'm reliable. I'm pliable. I'm easily swayed because I don't have strong enough views one way or the other.

Frank You seem to have quite strong views about this.

Michael That's precisely it. When you fall properly in love, it throws everything else into perspective.

Frank What are you on about?

Michael Ah, the great passion of my life! Shall I tell you?

Frank I'm intrigued, but you'll have to be quick; I'm on again soon. Is my hair OK?

Michael You've youthened a bit. Hold still.

Frank Ta.

Michael (*spraying Frank's hair with dry shampoo*) Yes, it's been preying on my mind for weeks now, ever since I read it again. I've always had a thing about it, even at school. Did it for O level, great stuff. And now it's all the stronger for having lain dormant all these years. I keep getting ideas, Frank, new ways of staging the scenes—insight into characters . . . there's a great production welling up inside me, and I'm damned if I'm not going to do it sooner or later.

Frank Must be quite some play. Let me guess . . . *Rookery Nook*?

Michael *Macbeth.*

Frank Michael! (*He jerks away, gaping at Michael, and gets spray on his face*)
Michael Sorry, I——
Frank Are you mad? We're in the middle of a show!
Michael What's the matter?
Frank And you go and mention——
Michael Oh, that! Surely you're not superstitious.
Frank Of course not, but there are limits. You can't go round spouting—that word, backstage. There's a curse on it. All the stories of people breaking their legs—even dying during productions of it . . . oh, for God's sake, get out of the room and come in again.
Michael Frank——
Frank Quick!
Michael Oh, if it'll keep you happy.

Michael goes out

Frank As if there haven't been enough disasters already tonight.

Michael returns

Michael All right, is that——
Frank Ah, ah, don't speak yet. Turn round three times.

Michael, gesturing in mockery, does so

Now swear.
Michael What?
Frank Any swear word.
Michael I've gone blank.
Frank Oh, bugger it, Michael——
Michael Bugger it!
Frank Thank God for that.
Michael I've never seen you like this before.
Frank That makes two of us. You've never struck me as the sort to harbour a grand passion.
Michael I suppose there's a first time for everyone. Do you want me to tell you some of the plans I've got——
Frank No! . . . Afterwards.
Michael As you wish. Oh, it's good to have someone to talk to about it.
Frank (*not wanting to hear*) Aha.
Michael I don't know why I've kept it bottled up . . . scared to have it all evaporate, I suppose, before it had . . . any real substance in my mind. But I'm confident now.
Frank That makes one of us.
Michael I'm sure I can do it, if I——
Frank Will you just shut up about it!
Michael Yes, yes. Sorry.
Frank Think of something else.
Michael OK . . . (*He tries to*) . . . Er . . . Oh, Lynne sends her love.

Frank Does she?

Michael Yes. I mean, to everyone.

Frank Ah! That's good. She coming to see the show?

Michael Yes, on Saturday. I tried to talk her out of it, but she's got this ludicrous sense of duty. Tonight and tomorrow she's just popping in at the end to whisk me away. Timing it so she doesn't get roped in for anything.

Frank Chauffeur service, eh?

Michael Oh, this is the new-look Michael and Lynne. It's called "making an effort".

Frank What is?

Michael We had a little meeting last week, Lynne and I. Sat down in the kitchen and thrashed things out.

Frank Sounds violent.

Michael She thought it was necessary.

Frank You don't have to tell me this, you know.

Michael No, I don't mind. The truth is, we've been going through what's known in the trade as a "bad patch".

Frank Oh, dear. I'm sorry.

Michael Lack of communication, getting on each other's nerves, long silences, icy glares, snide remarks—you know the sort of thing.

Frank I'll take your word for it.

Michael She reckoned we weren't giving it a chance. Not spending enough time together. Not sufficiently ... what's the word? (*He gestures*)

Frank Overacting?

Michael Demonstrative.

Frank Ah. Hence the chauffeur treatment.

Michael Yeah.

Frank God, I'd better go, I'm on in a second—— (*He starts to go*)

Michael She even told me she'd been on the brink of an affair.

Frank (*stopping suddenly*) Ah ... ! ... my goodness. Did she ... give any details?

Michael No. I don't want to know. Past history now. It's the future that counts. More effort, more togetherness, more ... em ... (*He gestures*)

Frank Demonstrations.

Michael And no acting for a while. Neither of us. We're to spend more time at home together. Apparently there's loads of decorating and gardening and things that need doing. She reckons we'd be better off if we gave the Thespians a miss for a year or so.

Frank I see. How do you feel about it?

Michael Well, I've hardly had a ball with this play, have I? And what's the programme for next year? Another West End comedy, an Agatha Christie, and a daring stab at a whole new genre ...

Frank } (*together*) *Blithe Spirit.*
Michael }

Michael And this November of course it's Bill's little ego trip.

Frank No, it's not.

Michael What?

Frank He's had to pull out, didn't you know?

Michael No, I didn't. So who's going to direct *Boeing-Boeing*?

Frank Nobody-nobody. Bill's always wanted to do it, so they're holding it over for him till the year after next. Treat to look forward to. His father's very ill, you know.

Michael Well, that's marvellous. They haven't got anyone else, have they?

Frank Not yet. There was talk of reviving *The Body in the Bidet*, but I can't see it myself.

Michael November. Well, it's a bit short notice, but . . .

Frank What are you thinking about?

Michael *Macbeth*, of course.

Frank turns on him

Frank Mich——

Sally rushes in

Sally Frank, for God's sake! You've missed your entrance!

Black-out. The sound of wind

After a short pause, the lights go up on the offices of Cooper & Dye. Front stage, an empty desk. Behind, a receptionist's desk, Jackie sitting at it with a typewriter in front of her, talking on the phone

Dye enters

Jackie (*on the phone*) Yes. . . . No, I'm sorry, 'e's still not in—can someone else be of assistance? . . . Righto, then, I'll tell 'im. . . . Thank you for callin'. (*She puts the phone down*)

Dye Dare I ask *who*'s still not in?

Jackie That was Mrs Dixon, she's rung twice already. (*She gives Dye some letters*) Some sort o' crisis with exchangin' contracts an' she wants Michael to sort it out. Says 'e seems the reliable type.

Dye He's fooled a lot of people that way.

Dye wanders away, looking through his letters. Jackie starts typing

Michael comes in stealthily

Jackie looks up and sees him, and is about to call to him when she sees he is trying to be inconspicuous. He sits at his desk. He shuffles some papers, then an idea comes to him and he gazes out front. Dye turns and sees him, and comes to behind his shoulder. He stands there for a while as Michael dreams

Fascinating, isn't it, that bit o' wallpaper?

Michael Oh! Hi, Les, hi. Just . . . er . . . working out a valuation. Property I saw yesterday.

Dye We pluck figures out o' the air these days, do we? I'm too old for this game, it's gettin' to be such a science.

Michael laughs

Late again, aren't you, Mikey?

Michael Am I? (*He looks at his watch*) Good God, yes . . . I really had no idea what time it——
Dye Save it, save it. Save it for when it's true. There's a young couple wants to see the showhouse on the Mountview Estate. Any offers? (*He looks round as if the office were full of people*) Er . . . Mikey. How about you?
Michael Sure, Les, sure. When?
Dye Seven o'clock.
Michael Ah . . . not this evening, I'm afraid . . . I'm in a play, if you remember.
Dye Ah, yes, yer amateur dramatics. Don't worry, I'll go meself.
Michael I'll work through my lunch hour, is that OK?
Dye I had a lunch hour once. A Thursday, it was. Lasted nearly five minutes.

Michael laughs

I 'spect you think I'm a workaholic, but you're wrong. I'm all in favour of lee-sure activities. Windin' down after the 'urly-burly of the day.
Michael "When the battle's lost and won."
Dye Eh?
Michael Nothing—it's just funny, that phrase you used——
Dye Tropical fish.
Michael Er . . .
Dye Me, it's tropical fish. My lee-sure activity. Sit an' look at 'em for hours, I can.
Michael Really.
Dye I once thought o' bringin' a tank to the office, brighten the place up, make a focal point, as they say. But I resisted the temptation. An' d'you know why, Mikey?
Michael I can't imagine.
Dye It's bad psychology. Here, sellin' properties. Home, tropical fish. Don't mix 'em. Business an' pleasure, keep 'em apart.
Michael I quite agree, Les.
Dye Course, in an ideal world, business would be a pleasure. (*He turns on him, cuttingly*) Wouldn't it?

Black-out. Sound of much animated conversation, as in a theatre bar. The lights come up on the bar in the church hall. The second performance of "A Bullet in the Back" has just finished; two or three members of the audience have stayed behind to drink with one another or the cast. To us, the members of the audience are invisible; all we see are the Thespians talking to them. The bar itself is just off-stage

Sally and Fiona are sitting at a table; Barnaby is talking to someone; another table is empty

Alan comes in with a pint, looks round, and heads straight for Sally and Fiona, passing Barnaby

Alan Hi, Barnaby. Done a good job?

Barnaby Oh, yeah, Alan. Fifty-seven tonight. That's five more than last night.

Alan Good stuff.

Barnaby Wasn't it great, eh? They all remembered all their lines, nearly.

Alan Yeah, an' some of 'em came in the right places too.

Barnaby You did the lightin' great.

Alan Thanks. Who's that bird with Sally?

Barnaby She's called Fiona. She's new. Ever so nice.

Alan See you, mate. (*He goes to join Sally and Fiona, and sits at their table*)

Geraldine enters, still in costume and make-up. She looks round the room as if searching for someone

Barnaby Oh, Geraldine! Well done, you were great!

Geraldine Thank you, Barnaby. Is the mayor still here?

Barnaby No, he had to leave at half-time. But he spoke to me before he went. He said it was a jolly good show and . . . what was it . . . you can all be very proud of yourselves. A jolly good show and you can all be very proud of yourselves.

Geraldine Did he single out anyone in particular?

Barnaby No, I don't think so.

Geraldine Typical. Jumped-up little socialist shopkeeper. Well, I may as well go and change, then.

Geraldine goes out

Sally He wants to do what?

Alan *Macbeth*. It's by some Midlands geezer, 'parently.

Sally I thought it was Shakespeare.

Fiona Course it is. We're not thick, you know.

Sally He's out of his mind.

Fiona Which one is Michael?

Sally The one who got murdered in the last act. Serious-looking bloke, with his flies undone.

Fiona Oh, him.

Sally I can't see him being much cop as a director. I've always seen Michael as a bloke who'd not got enough drive to get himself 'ome.

Alan You done much actin' yourself, Fiona?

Fiona Not a lot. Wouldn't mind being in something like *Macbeth*, though. Exciting.

Sally Borin', if you ask me. Long speeches an' blokes standin' around in tights.

Alan He's got lots of great ideas. Been tellin' me the sort o' set he wants——

Sally If we do it.

Fiona Oh, I hope we do. I liked it when we read it at school. I was Second Witch.

Alan Play your cards right, you might get First Witch this time. I have influence, you know.

Fiona gives him a bored grimace

See 'er ladyship just now?

Sally Could I miss 'er! Chargin' into the bar in full costume an' make-up.

Alan She's afraid of her fan-club rushin' off before she can squeeze the praise out of 'em.

Fiona Who's her ladyship?

Sally Bloody Geraldine. The big lady with the wig. She thinks she owns the Thespians.

Fiona She's certainly got presence.

Alan So would you if you were her size an' stood centre stage mouthin' everyone else's lines. Geraldine's the only person I know who can mask someone by standin' behind 'em.

Fiona You don't half think a lot of yourself, don't you?

Michael and Frank emerge, each carrying a pint. Michael also has a gin and tonic

Frank Who's the g and t for; Lynne?

Michael No, no. Wait and see.

They go to the empty table, where Barnaby intercepts them

Barnaby Well done, Frank—Michael. You were both great again tonight.

Frank Nice of you to say so, Barnaby. Got a drink?

Barnaby Oh, yes. (*He holds up an orange juice*) I'm making it last. Hey—I sold fifty-seven programmes tonight.

Frank Very good.

Barnaby Beats me how you remember all them lines.

Frank Question of having to, lad. You'll find that out when you get on stage yourself.

Barnaby Who, me?

Michael looks heavenward

Frank You never know.

Barnaby Oh, you can't see me on a stage! I mean—can you? Not that I wouldn't love to . . .

Frank You should have a go. We all had to start sometime.

Barnaby What a thought, eh! (*He laughs delightedly*) Oh—'scuse me—hey, Arnold . . . Arnold—you were great . . .

He scuttles off-stage

Michael Can you picture him on stage, Frank?

Frank Course. You'll need all the able-bodied men you can find if . . . your production goes ahead.

Michael Yes, but I'd rather they were able-minded as well.

Frank And what does Lynne have to say about it all?

Michael I . . . haven't got round to telling her yet.

Frank Oh? Is this part of the new communicative relationship?

Michael Just waiting for the right moment. It may not happen, after all. No sense in broaching it if it's a non-starter.

Frank P'raps not.

Michael But I'm damned if I'll let it not happen. I've sounded Alan out—
he's raring to go. And you're keen, aren't you?

Frank Oh, yes. It's a great idea. Ambitious, undeniably, but——

Michael So the only person I have to convince is Geraldine.

Frank Hold on. There's five of us on the committee. Sally, Henry, Geraldine, Arnold and me.

Michael So three's a majority. And have you ever known Arnold vote
against Geraldine?

Frank The mind boggles. She'd confiscate his keys.

Michael Exactly. So guess who the gin's for.

Frank You wily old sod.

Alan comes over to join them

Alan Hi, boss. Ta for the pint.

Michael That's OK, Alan.

Alan I'll get you one, shall I? Soon as I land myself a job. (*He sits*)

Michael You'll have a full-time job with *Macbeth*, my lad. (*To Frank*) It's
ideal, you know, Alan being unemployed. He'll be able to spend as much
time as he needs to on the show.

Alan That's me, boss, born lucky. Er . . . that new girl, Fiona. You know the
one, sittin' with Sally? She likely to get a part?

Michael I don't know yet. I've never even heard her speak.

Alan Oh, she's . . . got quite a tongue on 'er.

Sally I think he fancies you.

Fiona Sticks out like a sore thumb. I can't stand blokes like that, think
they're God's gift.

Sally Alan's all right.

Fiona What's he do, anyway?

Sally He's unemployed just at present. But he's ever so clever.

Fiona I bet he told you that.

Frank There's just one thing, Michael—do you think you could try to avoid
mentioning it by name?

Michael What, *Macbeth*?

Frank If you wouldn't mind.

Alan I thought that was only in the dressin'-room.

Frank Well, it's particularly dressing-rooms, but one really can't be too
careful.

Michael It's typical of amateur theatre, this. The only thing most people
learn from the pros are their camp terminology and their superstitions.

Frank Thanks very much.

Michael I've already had Eric screaming at me for mentioning it backstage.

Alan How can you put on a play without usin' its name? "The Shellsfoot
Thespians proudly present *Thingummy*"?

Frank The Scottish Play. You call it The Scottish Play. And the leading
character's called Scottish Person.

Michael Honestly!

Frank Please, Michael.

Michael What, on the posters, and the programme? And the name does come up occasionally in the course of the play, you know.

Frank Of course not, but wherever it's possible to avoid——

Geraldine returns

Michael Hold your horses, here she is.

Alan Oh, yeah. I thought the sun'd gone in.

Frank Michael, if she does agree to doing it, how in the world are you going to stop her playing ... er ...

Alan Lady Scottish Person.

Frank Quite.

Michael One step at a time, Frank. (*He calls*) Geraldine! Over here.

Geraldine Oh, hello.

Michael Gin and tonic all right for you?

Geraldine (*joining them*) My goodness. Yes, thank you. I did ask Arnold to get me one, but he appears to have forgotten.

Alan There goes next week's allowance.

Michael You know, if it hadn't been for you, Geraldine, we'd never have had a bar in this place at all.

Geraldine That's quite true. I'm glad it's not forgotten. The original plans were for a poky little place like the hall at St Martin's Westdale. But when I realized how useful it would be to the Thespians, I had a little chat with the vicar——

Alan From which he barely emerged with his life——

Geraldine And this is the result. A good-sized stage, lighting facilities that are the envy of every club in the area, and of course the bar.

Frank We owe a great deal to you and Arnold, Geraldine.

Geraldine I hesitate to attribute our influence to the small contributions we regularly make to the church fund ...

Frank I know the vicar has the highest regard for both of you.

Michael Is it true, by the way, that *Boeing-Boeing*'s been postponed?

Geraldine Yes; isn't it sad? We haven't a play or a director at the moment. I'm toying with the idea of directing myself; but I can't help feeling my real place is on the stage.

Michael I was wondering ... I have an ambition to direct something ...

Frank Careful, Michael.

Michael It's not the sort of thing we usually do, but I think we could make a success of it.

Geraldine Would I have heard of it?

Michael I hope so. It's Shakespeare.

Geraldine Ah. Not many good parts for women. Which play?

Michael *Macbeth*.

Geraldine Aaah! (*She rocks back in her chair, and almost falls off it*)

Frank The Scottish Play, that is, of course, Geraldine.

Geraldine Michael, are you insane? With one performance still to go, you mention that!

Michael I am sorry, I was forgetting.

Geraldine Turn around three times, for heaven's sake.

Michael gets up resignedly and turns round three times

Frank Hasn't he got to leave the room first?
Alan I thought it was only in the dressin'-room.
Geraldine No, no, three times, then spit.
Frank Spitting! I forgot that.

Michael spits into his empty glass

Geraldine Swear—but it needn't be a strong one. I usually say "dash it".
Michael Dash it.
Geraldine There.
Frank Doesn't he have to leave the room?
Geraldine Of course not. Why on earth should he do that?

Frank gestures with meek speechlessness

Michael Anyway. I was saying——
Frank Yes. It may seem like a strange idea at first, but just think about it,
Geraldine. It grows on you.
Geraldine The Scottish Play? Here?
Frank He's got some really original ideas, he's been telling me.
Geraldine With the Thespians?
Michael There's the old Magic Circle trick of using black velvet as a
backcloth. In certain lights, if you wear black, you can't be seen against it.
Geraldine The Scottish Play . . .
Michael That's for the witches and the apparitions. Then I'd like a small hill
to be built on one side of the set. The stage would have to be extended, of
course . . .
Frank It needn't be as expensive as it sounds.
Geraldine The Scottish Play . . .
Frank Of course, Michael wants your blessing before he thinks too deeply
about it. But wouldn't it be prestigious for the group? Our first Shakes-
peare?
Geraldine The Scottish Play . . .
Michael I can cast it virtually without thinking . . . certain people are
obvious for certain parts.
Frank Michael, for God's sake . . .
Geraldine (*suddenly, standing up*) "We fail? But screw your courage to the
sticking place, and we'll not fail!"
Frank (*applauding*) Bravo!
Geraldine I learned that speech in elocution lessons, you know. "When
Duncan is asleep . . ." and so on. You know, Michael, it's not nearly so
stupid an idea as it sounds.
Michael Thank you very much.
Geraldine "When in swinish sleep, their drenched natures lie as in a death,
what cannot you and I perform upon the something Duncan?"

Lynne comes in

Michael "Unguarded".

Lynne Oh, there you are, Mike.
Michael Oh! Oh, God . . . em . . . hi, darling. On our way, then? (*He gets up*)
Geraldine "What not put upon his spongy officers——"
Frank (*evenly*) Lynne. You're looking well.
Lynne (*evenly*) So are you, Frank.
Geraldine "Who dares receive it other, as we shall make our grief and clamour roar upon his death?"
Lynne Isn't it bad luck to go round quoting *Macbeth*?

Frank crosses himself

Michael Well, we'd better be going.
Geraldine We'll all be doing it soon, Lynne. Your clever husband! (*She pinches Michael's cheek*)
Michael I expect you're double-parked as usual, eh?
Lynne What's going on? Why is Michael suddenly clever?
Michael I'll tell you all about it when we——
Geraldine We're doing The Scottish Play in November, Lynne. Michael's directing it.
Michael It's not definite yet, of course——
Geraldine Oh, yes, it is.
Michael I was going to——
Lynne But that's lovely for you, Mike. You've always wanted to do it, haven't you?
Frank He really has got some wonderful ideas for it, Lynne.
Lynne Good. Well, you can tell me all about it when we get home. Better dash now, darling——
Michael Er . . . won't you stay for a drink?
Lynne No, it's getting late. I expect you're tired out. Bye, everyone.
Michael Er, right . . . good-night . . . see you tomorrow . . .

They all say good-night

Michael and Lynne leave

Geraldine "To bed, to bed; there's knocking at the gate . . . what's done cannot be undone . . ."
Alan (*indicating Michael and Lynne*) Somethin' tells me the drama's just about to begin.
Frank Poor chap, I hope she's lenient with him.
Geraldine To think, at last, Shakespeare at the Thespians! Oh, it's so exciting. So very exciting. I've been looking for something I could really get my teeth into . . .
Alan What's up with the glass you usually use?

Black-out

In the darkness, Frank speaks

Michael enters and stands front stage

Frank   Go bid thy mistress, when my drink is ready,

She strike upon the bell. Get thee to bed.
Is this a dagger which I see before me,
The handle toward my hand?

A light comes up on Michael's face; Frank is seen vaguely, in shadow

Michael Now, is there to be a real dagger? Does the audience see it, or is it just in Macbeth's imagination?

Frank (*reaching in front of him*) . . . a dagger of the mind, a false creation, Proceeding from the heat oppressèd brain?

During Michael's next speech, Frank slips away

Michael Yes, that's right. There *shouldn't* be a real dagger. The witches were real, the apparitions later are real, so the audience sees them too. But this is Macbeth's own creation, just like the Ghost of Banquo at the feast . . . *he* sees them, but *we* don't.

The lights snap up—we are in Michael's and Lynne's lounge, and he has a bowl of cereal in his hand. She is seething. Without speaking, she picks up some cereal off the floor where he has dropped it, and plops it back into his bowl. Then she goes to the sofa and sits there with a newspaper. He looks at her helplessly

Lynne, I *am* sorry . . .

Lynne Aha.

Michael I was meaning to tell you——

Lynne Oh, good.

Michael I just didn't seem to find the right moment . . .

Lynne No.

Michael Honestly . . . you were the sixth . . . seventh person to know . . .

Lynne Really.

Michael Well, I've said I'm sorry, and . . . what more can I say?

Lynne (*softening a little*) Mike, you are silly. Of course you've got to do *Macbeth* if there's an opportunity. You've always wanted to, you can't throw away the chance. What hurts me is that you didn't tell me. Why didn't you tell me?

Michael I . . . I suppose I thought you might make difficulties.

Lynne Then you don't understand me. Or you think I'm some sort of ogre. I don't make difficulties when there's no reason. I might have presented you with a few pros and cons to think about, because knowing you they won't have crossed your mind. Is that what you were afraid of?

Michael I don't know.

Lynne But to hear about it by accident, and from Geraldine of all people! How do you think I felt?

Michael I can still do the decorating, you know, and gardens don't grow in autumn——

Lynne Who told you that?

Michael They don't, do they?

Lynne You won't have the time. And you certainly won't have the energy.

It's far more sapping than being in a play, you know. I did some directing at college—it's bloody hard work. But I've told you, it doesn't really matter. It's not jobs around the house that were the real problem, anyway. It's more an attitude, it's a way of thinking about us. I can get started on the painting—it'll be easier with you out of the way. I might even run to sticking up a few rolls of wallpaper.

Michael But you can't.

Lynne No, it's *you* that can't do wallpaper——

Michael I don't mean that. I mean . . . you're going to be Lady Macbeth.

Lynne Oh! Thanks for telling me.

Michael Well, of course you are. Who else could play the part?

Lynne (*after a deep breath*) In the first place, there's something called auditions——

Michael Formality.

Lynne In the second place, you can't go round giving the leading part to your own wife.

Michael If I'm directing the play——

Lynne Third, I'd like to get at least the lounge decorated by Christmas, and fourth why the hell didn't you ask me?

Michael I suppose I took it for granted.

Lynne Exactly!

Michael I'm asking you now.

Lynne (*exasperated*) Ohhh! (*She gets up and crosses the room*) Who's Macbeth, anyway? I s'pose that's all sewn up. (*She turns*) You're not thinking of doing it yourself?

Michael No, don't be silly.

Lynne Thank God for *small* mercies.

Michael Frank, of course.

Lynne Oh! I see. Well, that settles it. I couldn't possibly be Lady Macbeth in that case.

Michael I thought you liked Frank.

Lynne (*as if explaining to a child*) Yes. But what would people say if you gave the two leads to your wife and your best friend?

Michael I don't care what people say. He's head and shoulders above the rest of them. He's the right age, he's got the build for it . . . he can speak verse, he's done Shakespeare before. And no-one else approaches him for sensitivity and intelligence . . . let alone his dedication to the job . . .

Lynne (*icily*) Perhaps you ought to have married Frank.

Michael (*sitting down*) Then the two of you—you act so well together. Remember *Separate Tables*? There's a definite rapport there, there's a chemistry . . .

Lynne, unseen by him, throws up her hands with a silent scream

I keep thinking of Two: Two, Macbeth and Lady Macbeth. You know the bit I mean?

The lights start to dim

Whenever I think of it, it's your voices I can hear. The great warrior—

deep, resonant voice—but just at this point it's wavering a little, he's not sure of himself. And she's got no fears, no doubts. A light, feminine voice, but strong as steel.

The lights go down to black-out, except for a spotlight on Michael's face

She won't bend like Macbeth in all the violent winds. Eventually, though—she'll snap.

Lynne He is about it:
The doors are open; and the surfeited grooms
Do mock their charge with snores: I have drugged their possets
That death and nature do contend about them,
Whether they live or die . . .

Michael Then suddenly the lights change, and everything's bathed in crimson. Red.

The light suddenly becomes red. Lynne as Lady Macbeth is seen in shadow

The whole forestage lit as if by luminous blood. The murder is done.

Frank enters, as Macbeth

Throughout the rest of the terrified, terrible scene, the crimson light remains. She goes to gild the faces of the grooms with Duncan's blood . . .

Lynne goes out

And then the knocking starts.

A regular series of knocks on a great door begins

Every few seconds, three steady knocks. Louder each time. A hopeless, heart-rending prayer:

Frank Wake Duncan with thy knocking! I would thou couldst! (*He moves to one side of the stage*)

Michael The red light concentrates, upstage, on the porter's brazier . . .

Barnaby emerges, carrying a small table that glows red in the prevailing light

Drunken, red-faced, red-lit, he warms his hands at the flames of hell. The forestage now in shadow, and the knocking goes on . . .

Eric (*speaking the porter's lines; they sound as if they come from the shadowy figure of Barnaby*) Here's a knocking indeed! If a man were porter of hell-gate, he should have old turning the key . . .

The knocking continues; the lights go up. No pause, but Barnaby takes over the speech. He is standing next to the table, innocuous in the new light, in the centre of the stage. We are in the church hall; at the auditions. Michael is sitting on a chair behind a table, with another chair beside it, on one side of the stage; on the other side are a few other people sitting or standing—Frank, Alan, Fiona, Sally and Eric. It is clear as the scene progresses that they are not the only ones there—the hall stretches beyond the stage, and there are other auditionees off-stage

Barnaby (*reading slowly and painfully*) Knock, knock, knock! Who's there, ith name of Beel ... Beez ... Beeble-zub? Here's a farmer, that hanged himself on thex—pec—tation of plenty——
Michael Thanks, Barnaby, that'll do.
Barnaby Oh, I—I thought it was the whole speech.
Michael Yeah, I think we can leave it there. There're enough murders in this play as it is.
Barnaby Right!

Quite happy, he walks over to Frank. Michael makes notes

Frank Well done, lad.
Barnaby I don't think he liked me much.
Frank You can never tell with Michael.
Barnaby I couldn't do a part like that, though. I'd never learn it. Just a tiny bit, that's what I want. Just to be on the stage, with Michael directing me. He's so clever, isn't he?
Sally Wonder where Lynne is? I thought she was tryin' for Lady M.
Alan An' 'ere's me thinkin' you'd poisoned 'er.
Fiona Poisoned?
Sally He's just bein' funny.
Fiona Oh, thanks for telling me.
Sally Lynne might speak posher than me, but I've always thought I've got more feeling than she has. More sort o' natural talent. And she's never 'ad much of what you'd call presence.
Alan Specially tonight.
Fiona Don't you ever stop joking?
Alan I'm tryin' to relax yer nerves, pet. Help you feel better.
Fiona Try falling under a bus.
Michael Right! I think I've heard as much as I need from everybody now, and I've got a pretty good idea of the casting, but ... er ... if you'd like to hold on just a few more minutes—Alan, can I have a word?
Alan Sure, boss. (*He crosses to Michael*)
Sally I feel sick.
Fiona Me too.
Barnaby Frank, this servant, in Act Three. Is that the smallest part in the play?
Frank Let's have a look. Well, couldn't get much smaller.
Barnaby That's the part I want, then. Act Three Scene Two, Lady ... Scottish Person ... enters with a servant.
Frank Good lad, you remembered.
Barnaby And I think you should play Scottish Person.
Alan Well, what d'you reckon? Can you cast it?
Michael Just about. But it means giving parts to people like Walter ... and Barnaby, God forbid.
Alan What 'bout your missis, in't she comin'?
Michael Oh, Lynne'll do Lady Macbeth. She doesn't want to, but she'll do it. There's no viable alternative, anyway. The one thing I'm really grateful for is Geraldine not turning up. I can't imagine why she hasn't, but it lets

me off lightly. I wasn't looking forward to her reaction to the cast list.
Alan You got a part for ... er ... Fiona?
Michael Oh, yeah. Second Witch.
Alan Great. Be fun strikin' 'er with lightnin'.
Michael What I was going to ask you—you know that other group you used to belong to?
Alan St Luke's?
Michael Yeah. Any good men there?
Alan Can you do that?
Michael I can do what I like. The object is to get a good cast for the play. I'd use professionals if we could run to it.
Alan Well, there's a couple of blokes I see down the pub now an' then. I'll sound 'em out, if you think it's kosher.
Michael If they're any good, I'll hear them. (*To everyone*) Right!
Sally I'm goin' to be sick.
Michael Before I read out the cast, there's just one thing I want to say.
Sally Oh, God.
Michael I want you to realize what sort of a commitment you're taking on. This is a very difficult play. Very few of you have done anything of this period before, and you've made it quite clear to me tonight that there'll need to be a lot of work done on your verse-speaking. For most shows we rehearse two nights a week. Well, for *Macbeth*——

Frank crosses himself

—it'll be four nights, seven-thirty till ten, and every Sunday afternoon from three till six. If that's not acceptable to anyone, please will they tell me now.

There is muttering. He surveys the assembly

Sally What, an' never know what part I was gonna get?
Frank Clever lad.
Michael Great; you're all behind me. There's no backing out now! This is the cast, then. It's not absolutely final, but I'll let you know any changes as soon as I can.
Fiona What does he mean by that?
Michael Macbeth——

Frank crosses himself

Geraldine bursts in

Geraldine So sorry I'm late, Michael dear. I couldn't get away. We're at a dinner party tonight, but it's friends of Arnold's I can't stand, so he stayed and I came over, just for a few minutes. It's only right that I should go through the motions of an audition—the same rules for everyone! But Arnold simply couldn't, it would have looked too bad if we'd both walked out on them. Anyway, he would like to double Porter and Duncan. My idea, actually. You don't need to hear him for that, do you?
Michael Actually, Geraldine——

Geraldine Now, what shall I do? I was thinking of the sleepwalking scene, if you're agreeable. Perhaps Frank could read in the doctor and Sally the gentlewoman—I expect she'll be playing it anyway.

She grabs Frank and Sally and positions them

Michael Geraldine——

Geraldine I've always envisaged this scene as taking place on a staircase, Lady Scottish Person standing on the top stair with her arms stretched out to heaven——

Alan Like King Kong on the Empire State Building.

Geraldine climbs on a chair and begins. Michael rests his head in his hands

Geraldine "Out, damnèd spot! Out, I say!

The lights go down

    All but Geraldine and Michael exit

Geraldine continues her speech; Michael is now seated at a table in one room of his house, with a model of the "Macbeth" set and chessmen to represent the characters. When there is total darkness, Geraldine stops; Lynne, who has entered, takes over the speech. The light will come up first on Michael, hearing Lynne's voice in his head, and Lynne, actually reading the speech in another part of the house, with a copy of the play in her hands. The two lit areas are separated by darkness

    One: two: why, then, 'tis time to do't. Hell is murky! Fie, my lord, fie! A soldier, and afeard? What need we fear who knows it——

Lynne —when none can call our power to account."

A light comes up on Michael

Michael Pause just a little for the searing effect of the next line——

    Geraldine exits

A light comes up on Lynne

Lynne Yet who would have thought the old man to have had so much blood in him?

Michael And the doctor steps back, almost struck dumb by the revelation. "Do you mark that?" (*He moves one of the chessmen*)

Lynne The Thane of Fife had a wife, where is she now?

There is a ring at the door. Michael does not react

    Oh, that'll be her. (*She calls*) Don't worry, Mike, I'll get it.

She goes out, and we hear a door opening

    (*Off*) Oh, hello.

Frank (*off*) Evening.

Lynne (*off*) Won't you come in?

Frank (*off*) Thanks.

Door closes, off

Frank and Lynne enter

Lynne I suppose you're wanting to see the Master.

Frank He's not here, is he?

Lynne Yes, he is. Bodily, anyway, he's in the dining-room. But if you want to enter his plane of existence, you'd better start sleepwalking or dress up as a tree.

Frank I thought he was going to see Alan tonight. Working on a model of the set.

Lynne That's all been done! Alan brought it round this morning—he was so keen he spent all night on it. I must say it's very impressive.

Frank Good old Alan.

Lynne And I've never seen Mike so happy. He's been playing with that model ever since he got in. I had to stop him taking it to work with him.

Frank I was like that with my first dog.

Lynne How old were you?

Frank Eight.

Michael The doctor's a timid man, quite out of his depth—an ordinary person swept up in great and bloody deeds.

Lynne He's plotting all the moves with chessmen. You're the black king and I'm the black queen.

Frank Ha.

Lynne So it isn't Mike you've come to see.

Frank Not exactly, no.

Lynne Well, that narrows the field. Sit down, won't you? I've made some coffee.

Frank Thanks, but, er ...

Lynne What is it?

Frank looks towards the dining-room

Don't worry about him, he's safely tucked up in Scotland.

Michael I don't want any of the old stately Mrs Siddons business of plodding across the stage with her candle in the air like a priest in a procession. She's agitated—darting this way and that—even coming right up to the doctor and addressing him directly. (*He moves a chess piece*)

Lynne It is a new side to him—I've never known him get so absorbed in anything. With the possible exception of me.

She pours him some coffee and they sit together

Frank Thanks. I take it from your presence at rehearsal last night that you're definitely doing the part.

Lynne What choice did I have? It was another *fait accompli*, wasn't it? If I'd refused, he'd have been miserable, looked silly and made life hell for me.

Frank And we'd probably have had Sally as Lady Scottish Person. Or Geraldine, of course.

Lynne That thought did cross my mind. Tell me, how *did* Geraldine take the news?

Frank She was so flabbergasted, or angry, or something, I don't think she could trust herself to speak. She just stood there for a while with a white face and her mouth open—then she turned and stormed out.

Lynne Didn't Mike say anything to her?

Frank Oh, yes—he told her that her style of acting wasn't suitable for Shakespeare—you know how tactful he is. Then as she was leaving he called out: "Oh, Geraldine, could you tell Arnold the first rehearsal's seven-thirty sharp on Tuesday."

Lynne Poor old bag.

They laugh

Frank So here we are.

Lynne The jolly old butcher and his fiend-like queen.

Frank So much for our determination to keep apart.

Lynne Indeed so.

Pause

Frank And what are we going to do?

Lynne Be little professionals, I suppose. Act the parts and forget everything else.

Frank It's not easy. I can do passionate scenes with people I quite like, or even with people I can't stand, but with you——

Lynne You did OK last night.

Frank It may not have been affecting my acting, love, but it was killing me. (*He takes her hand*)

Lynne (*withdrawing her hand*) Please.

Frank That's what I mean. If Scottish bugger's allowed to, why can't I?

Lynne It should have been a cleaner break, shouldn't it? One of us should have left the group altogether.

Frank For what ostensible reason? We've been through all that. No. I can't help thinking that fate or something's trying to tell us——

Lynne I don't want to hear that sort of nonsense. I made my choice a while back, and I haven't changed my mind. You've allowed yourself to forget that I still love Michael, and that he's your friend as well, and that neither of us wants to hurt him.

Frank Yes. I'm sorry.

Lynne I hope you didn't come round here expecting anything else.

Frank I didn't, no. I came round to make sure that you *were* intending to play the part. And, if you were, to give you prior warning that I'm going to drop out.

Lynne Oh, no.

Frank One of us has to, and you can't.

Lynne But for Macbeth——

Frank Lynne!

Lynne wheels round, as if Michael has come in

Lynne What?—Oh, I'm sorry—em—Scottish Person. That's too much of a sacrifice, Frank.

Frank Not really. You know me and acting. It's not exactly in my blood, the way it is with some people. I may have a bit of a talent for it, but I've got other interests. To tell you the truth, I don't relish the prospect of spending four nights a week between now and November hanging around a draughty church hall. Not even for Scottish Person.

Lynne So what are you going to say to Mike?

Frank I can cobble together some plausible story about business commitments. I'll give him a ring at the office in the next few days.

Lynne I suppose it's the only thing we can do. He'll be very upset.

Frank Cruel to be kind. Right then.

Lynne Yes.

Frank Better be going. (*He takes her hand, squeezes it, and does not let go*)

Lynne S'pose so.

Frank Or . . .

Lynne "At once, good-night. Stand not upon the order of your going, but go at once."

Michael suddenly gets up from his table, and walks into their room, carrying and reading his book. He pours himself a cup of coffee and returns to the dining-room, ignoring Lynne and Frank, who are still holding hands

I've made up my mind not to get really worried until I see him rubbing his hands.

Black-out. Wind. Then the noise of a pub at closing time takes over, with a landlord calling "time". The lights go up on a table in a pub, and Sally, Fiona and Barnaby in the process of sitting down at it, with their drinks

Sally Only just made it.

Barnaby Shouldn't we get drinks for Michael and the others?

Sally No. At this rate they won't be through rehearsin' till gone eleven. He's turned out a real slave driver—I'd never have thought it.

Fiona You can't tell with these introvert types, can you?

Sally And talk about inconsiderate. You know Bob's 'ad to miss 'is darts match to come to rehearsal? Well, he's been stuck in there since half-seven, and Mike's not even got to 'is scene yet.

Fiona I didn't think you were called tonight, Barnaby?

Barnaby No, I wasn't. But I wasn't doing anything else. I like coming along—you sort of get more involved, don't you, the more you watch.

Sally If you say so.

Barnaby An'—like tonight—I mean, Terry didn't turn up, did he? Someone had to read his lines in.

Fiona Yeah, Michael did.

Barnaby Well, he *could* have chosen me. But—he couldn't have done if I hadn't been there.

Sally You're really into it, aren't you, love?

Fiona Oh, no.

Sally What?

Fiona Lighting person.

Sally Oh, Fiona, he's not so bad.

Fiona He's not after you, is he? Honestly, makes me sick. Every time he

opens his mouth he comes out with some stupid joke, then he looks at me
to see if I'm impressed. I can't stand these men who just talk and never *do*.

Sally Well——

Fiona All he has to do is flick a few switches, doesn't he? There's no skill.

Alan (*off*) Bollocks.

Fiona Oh, good, they won't serve him.

Alan enters with the model of the set for "Macbeth"

Alan Hi, kids, I was gonna top you up, but they've stopped servin'.

Fiona Shame.

Barnaby You can have mine, Alan.

Alan (*looking at Barnaby's orange juice*) That's OK, mate.

Fiona There's lots of empty tables over there.

Alan (*sitting*) You know, that's what I like about you, Fiona. You're so
informative. Always handy with a choice morsel o' conversation.

Sally We was just sayin' how hard Mike's workin' everyone. There's ever
such a lot of grumblin' already.

Barnaby Steve says he's going to pull out—and he's got thirty-eight lines.

Sally There's another thing—Mike hasn't a clue about budgeting. I tried to
pin him down tonight to some figures, but he's so vague. "Wait an' see,"
he kept sayin'. An' he's never heard of the word "economy". I said to
him, what about usin' some of the costumes we already got—that'll save a
few quid. I mean, that last pantomime, the men were all dressed up in a
sort o' soldier's gear, an' all the women had old-fashioned dresses—they'd
do for this show, wouldn't they? He got really ratty.

Alan No imagination, that's 'is trouble.

Fiona Hey, what're you doing with that model?

Alan I'm takin' it 'ome with me. Start work on the lightin' tonight.

Fiona I hope you're careful with it, then. There's a lot of work gone into
that.

Alan You don't say.

Sally Alan did make it, you know.

Fiona What?

Alan Yeah. Who did you think?

Fiona Well, I thought ... Michael ...

Alan Na. He's an ideas man. His idea of DIY's knockin' nails in with a
screwdriver.

Sally D'you remember once when we was set-buildin' round at Brian's
place, an' Mike was sawin' up strips of 'ardboard on Brian's kitchen
table?

Alan Yeah. We're still usin' bits o' that table.

Fiona But it's ever so clever, this model. Really ... intricate.

Alan Yeah, 's one o' me best.

Fiona All these different bits of curtain, the way they all pull across.

Alan It 'elps when I'm designin' the lights, I can see just where the sightlines
are.

Sally You wait till you see the real thing.

Fiona Who builds the set, then?

Sally Well, everybody helps out, but Alan's in charge. It's quite an operation.
Fiona Oh! You never said.
Alan Thought everyone knew. Well, if there's no booze, I better get on 'ome. 'E wants the lightin' plot done by tomorrer.
Sally Blimey.
Alan See y'all, then. (*He gets up*)
Sally Night, Alan.
Barnaby Good-night!
Fiona (*reflective*) Yeah, good-night.

Alan leaves

Sally He's a scream. It's funny to see 'im with Michael. I don't think Mike'd know a joke if it fell on 'im.
Barnaby Will you test me on these lines, Sally?
Sally OK, love. Started learning it already, have you?
Barnaby (*giving her his book*) It's from the top of the page.
Sally Right.
Barnaby "Doubtful it stood, as two spent swimmers——"
Sally Hey, hold on. This isn't you, it's the bleedin' Captain, Scene One. That's Brian's part.
Barnaby I know. But I thought I'd learn it anyway, just in case. You never know, do you?

Sally stares at him

"Doubtful it stood, as two spent swimmers that do cling together——

The lights begin to fade to black-out

—and choke their art, the merciless Macdonwald worthy to be a rebel for to that the multiplying villainies of nature do swarm upon him ..."

Complete black-out. Then lights come up on the offices of Cooper & Dye. Jackie is at her desk, typing. Dye is at his desk, reading and making notes. Michael is at his desk, on the phone, but keeping his voice down

Michael Look, Terry, I don't care where you've got to go tomorrow morning, or what time you've got to get up.

Dye stands and comes into Michael's office

You'll be there at rehearsal tonight, or you're out of the—hello? Terry? Oh, bloody idiot. (*He puts the phone down*)
Dye I hope that wasn't a client, Mikey?
Michael No, Les, no. Em ... vendor's solicitors.
Dye I see. (*He picks up a book from Michael's desk*) You know, Cooper an' Dye's really goin' up in the world.
Michael Em, Les——
Dye But I wish you'd keep me informed. When were we instructed to sell this desirable property?
Michael It's just something I was——

Dye "This castle hath a pleasant seat; the air nimbly and sweetly recommends itself unto our gentle senses ..." Bit old-fashioned, that, Mikey. An' I don't think our clients need to know about the birds nestin' in the gutters.

Michael I brought it in to read during my lunch hour.

Dye Lunch hour! You're 'aving a lunch hour!

Michael Well——

Dye Since you deigned to arrive this mornin' at thirteen minutes past ten, I assumed you intended to work through your lunch hour. Again.

Michael Well ... OK. Yes, of course.

Dye Yes, of course. Now, about this evening. Young bloke, first-time buyer——

Michael Not tonight, I'm afraid, Les.

Dye Your little play again.

Michael 'Fraid so.

Dye All right. If you've made a commitment, you've made a commitment. I'm not a tyrant; I've told you that before. But I would be grateful if you didn't make so many commitments.

Michael Just at present, I'm——

Dye I used to say about you, with regard to estate agency: not much feel for it, not much flair, an' 'e doesn't seem to like the job. An' there's the odd week when he can't work evenin's 'cos of 'is dramatics. But, all in all, he's someone you can depend on. He's solid, he's reliable, an' he's always *there*.

Michael Thank you.

Dye But I'm not sayin' that now, Mikey. You're *not* always there. And even when you are there, you're not.

Michael I——

Dye Buck your ideas up, my lad, or you'll 'ave them bucked up for you. An' for the next few weeks, do me a favour, will you? Keep yer evenin's free. (*He goes away*)

Michael But, Les, I ... oh, God. (*He takes out some house details and starts to read them*)

Geraldine enters, going to Jackie's desk

Jackie Can I 'elp you, madam?

Geraldine I've seen what I want, thank you. (*She approaches Michael's desk and sits by it*)

Michael (*gloomily*) Yes. What can I do for you? (*He looks up*) Oh, God!

Geraldine (*sweetly*) You won't sell many houses that way, Michael.

Michael Oh ... you're ... you're wanting a house, are you?

Geraldine No, it's Thespian business I've come about.

Michael looks furtively behind him

Michael Er ... could we possibly postpone this till some other time ... they're not very keen on personal callers here.

Geraldine It won't take long. I was speaking to Sally this morning.

Committee business. She tells me there are problems over the budget for The Scottish Play.

Michael Oh, one or two. But it's nothing we can't solve. She's just got to be more realistic, that's all. Not expect to keep cutting corners. You can't do a play like this without spending a bit of money on it ... and I don't believe in just making do.

Geraldine I quite agree with you. Unfortunately not everyone's such a perfectionist, or so dedicated to the Thespians.

Michael I don't know about being dedicated to the Thespians, but I certainly want this production to be successful. As successful as I can possibly make it. And if that means spending a bit of money, then so be it.

Geraldine However, money doesn't grow on trees.

Michael I've told Sally to organize some fund-raising events. Jumble sales, raffles, that sort of thing. Some people just won't get off their backsides to make an effort.

Geraldine I was wondering if I could be of any service.

Michael Were you?

Geraldine Arnold and I have a little money put by for worthy causes. I think this is as worthy as any.

Michael Really?

Geraldine Don't you?

Michael Oh, yes, of course, but ... well!

Geraldine Do you think five hundred pounds would help?

Michael Are you serious?

Geraldine We don't really expect to recoup it, of course. But simply the pleasure of knowing that we have contributed to something worthy and excellent.

Michael I must say, Geraldine, this is really very good of you. I couldn't have imagined ... well ...

Geraldine If I write out a cheque now, you can take it straight to your bank.

Michael My bank?

Geraldine If Sally got her hands on it, she might create difficulties. I'm sure I can trust you to spend it on The Scottish Play.

Michael Yes. Fine. Thank you.

Geraldine gets out her cheque book and a pen and starts writing

Geraldine Of course, there are certain things that need to be ironed out, but I'm sure we can come to an arrangement.

Michael Yes. (*After a pause*) What certain things?

Geraldine I was talking to the vicar yesterday. He was very surprised at some of the casting.

Michael Was he?

Geraldine Several of my friends have expressed the same view.

Michael Well, you can't please——

Geraldine In fact, Mrs Pendleton was quite indignant. She thought I was born to play Lady Scottish Person.

Michael Geraldine, if this is some sort of——

Geraldine Especially since I have been such a loyal supporter of the

Thespians ever since it was founded. One of the keystones, the vicar says.
Michael The casting's been done. I'm not going to change my mind.
Geraldine And so much of our money has already found its way into the coffers——
Michael If you think you can twist my arm by offering me——
Geraldine Well, here's the cheque. What do you say?

She holds it up to him. He takes it, but she doesn't let go

Michael Thank you.
Geraldine And——?
Michael I'm sorry, Geraldine. I'm still not going to give you the part. I'm sure we can find the money somehow, without compromising the production.
Geraldine But you virtually promised it to me, that night in the bar.
Michael I'm sorry if you got that impression.
Geraldine You deliberately misled me to secure my approval.
Michael I did nothing of the——
Geraldine You can't run this group like the National Theatre, you know. In Amateur Dramatics there are certain loyalties that must be——
Michael I hate that phrase "Amateur Dramatics". It sounds like kids playing at dressing up and talking in silly voices. This is an artistic enterprise, we're just not getting paid for it, that's all. What the hell's the point of putting on a play like *Macbeth* if you start compromising all over the place?
Geraldine You can't treat my theatre group as if it were a ... a ...
Michael *Your* theatre group!
Geraldine A temple for the glorification of you and your silly little wife!
Michael (*hissing*) Well, it's better than being a resting place for superannuated old hams!

Geraldine is rendered speechless and glares. Dye approaches

Dye Everything all right here?
Michael Yes, Les. Mrs Hopkinson's just going ... aren't you? (*He picks up a pile of house details*) This one might be worth a look, and ... er ... oh, yes, these ... em ... very suitable to your needs.

She takes the papers, still fixing him with a glare

Dye (*intercepting the papers*) I'm sure Mrs 'Opkinson doesn't need five copies of thirty-seven Cowper Street, 'owever suitable to 'er needs.
Michael Oh ... oh ... my mistake ... em ...
Dye 'As my assistant been givin' satisfactory assistance, Mrs 'Opkinson?
Michael The trouble is, there's just not much available in her range, just at present. Shall I ... show you out, madam? (*He takes her by the arm*)
Dye Don't man'andle the clients, Mikey.

Geraldine stops, shakes off Michael's arm, and turns to him

Geraldine You are an ignorant, incompetent and offensive young man. I can only trust you get the comeuppance you deserve. (*Grandly*) But there is one thing you will not get, and that is Arnold. Good-morning.

Dye Goodbye, Mrs 'opkinson! 'Ope you call again!

She sweeps out

There is a pause

Michael Les . . .

Dye Now, the question is——

Michael I can explain——

Dye —are you an ignorant, incompetent and offensive estate-agent, or was that——

Michael It was a personal visit.

Dye I suppose that's a relief. At least it saves me askin' you who Arnold is, an' what you'd have done with 'im if you'd been allowed to 'ave 'im.

Michael There was nothing I could do. She just barged in; I couldn't——

Dye Business and pleasure, Mikey, you know what my views are.

Michael Pleasure.

Dye Com-part-mentalize. Work is work and play is play. A place for everything, and everything in its place. We sell properties. Sell some!

Dye goes back to his desk. Jackie's phone rings and she answers it

Michael Yes, Les. Sorry, Les. Bastard. (*He picks up some leaflets and shuffles them. His phone rings*) Yeah?

Jackie Frank for you, Mike.

Michael Oh . . . tell him I'll ring back.

Jackie He says it's urgent.

Michael God . . . OK.

Frank is lit, in another part of the stage

Jackie puts her phone down

(*Quietly*) Hi, Frank.

Frank Michael.

Michael Keep it short, the natives are hostile.

Frank Right . . . It's . . . a bit difficult, really. I'm going to have to pull out of the play.

Michael (*loudly*) What! (*Quietly*) You're joking.

Frank No, I'm sorry. It's my firm, you see. They're sending me abroad—to the States. The week of the production.

Michael Well, tell them you can't go.

Frank It's not as easy as that. There's nobody else they could send. I'm bloody sick, I can tell you.

Michael *You're* bloody sick! You can't drop out. It's as simple as that— you're indispensable.

Frank I'm sure one of the others would do a good job if you helped them along. It's about time someone else had a chance, anyway. I'm always playing leads.

Michael I don't care about "always" or giving people chances. It's *Macbeth* we're talking about—

Frank crosses himself

—and that's the part you're playing.

Frank I can't do it, Michael. My boss doesn't understand things like commitments to plays. Well, surely you can appreciate that?

Michael Would you like me to have a word with him?

Frank (*hurriedly*) No. I don't think that would do any good. Honestly, I have done my best. If I'd tried any harder, they'd have thought I lacked dedication.

Michael You do, I could tell them that.

Frank To my job, I mean. They'd think I wasn't ... you know ... promotion material.

Michael So what? So bloody what? (*He slams the phone down*)

The light on Frank goes out. Michael walks across the room, and yells

Amateurs!

Dye wheels round and stares at him. Black-out

ACT II

The church hall

Michael and Lynne come in. Michael is in a foul mood. Lynne is fighting to tolerate him. He switches the light on. There is no one there. He looks at his watch, then stands waiting, in an aggressive pose. Lynne takes off her coat, wanders across the hall, looks at things, sits down, reads her script. Michael looks at his watch again

Michael Right! So where *is* everyone? (*He swings round and almost collides with . . .*)

Barnaby, who has just rushed in

Barnaby Sorry I'm late, Michael.

Lynne You're not, Barnaby, it's exactly half-past.

Michael Only the fourth rehearsal, and already everyone's late!

Barnaby D'you want me to read in——?

Michael Where the bloody hell *are* they all? (*He starts mapping out the acting area with chalk or string, and placing items of furniture*)

Lynne It's no use shouting at us, Mike. We're the goody-goodies, we're here on time. Don't take any notice of him, Barnaby; he's upset because Frank's dropped out.

Barnaby Frank? Oh, no! What are we going to do?

Lynne Well, some of us have responded by throwing a wobbly. It remains to be seen whether this brings about a solution to the problem.

Alan comes in

Alan Hi, boss.

Michael You're late.

Alan starts helping Michael

Alan Got a couple o' bits o' news for you.

Michael What's that?

Alan First thing, those three blokes from St Luke's you met the other night. They'll do the parts, if you still want 'em.

Michael Oh, thank God for that.

Lynne Three blokes? You don't need three more men, Mike.

Michael Yes, I do, even more now. What's the other news?

Alan Oh, nothing much. I got a job.

Lynne Oh, Alan, well done!

Michael When does it start?

Alan Not till after the show, I made sure of that.

Michael That's OK, then. (*He wanders away, studying his script*)

Sally and Fiona come in

Lynne I'm very pleased, Alan. So's Mike, really, but he's a bit—well, you know.

Alan Yeah.

Lynne What sort of job is it, anyway?

Alan Theatre. General dogsbody, changing the bog rolls, that sort o' thing. But it's a start.

Lynne It certainly is. Oh, I'm so pleased. Did you hear that, Mike?

Mary comes in

Michael What sort of bloody time do you think this is?

Mary It's only just gone half-seven. You haven't started yet.

Michael I couldn't bloody start, could I?

Mary There's no need to swear.

Lynne (*going over to him; in a hissing whisper*) Mike, will you control your——

Frank comes in

Michael and Lynne stare at him. The others, who hadn't heard that he'd dropped out, stare at Michael and Lynne. Frank waves sheepishly, and goes into a corner with his book. Michael marches over to him

Barnaby It's Frank!

Michael What are you doing here?

Frank I suppose you could say you broke down my defences. I went crawling to my boss and begged him to change the date of the American trip. After half an hour of pleading and a mouthful of boot-polish, I finally got him to relent.

Michael Thank God for that!

Frank I'm not exactly his favourite person at the moment.

Michael Oh, but!—Tell you what, Frank. He can have a free ticket for the show, any night he likes. No, what the hell—two!

Lynne (*who has come to join them*) Careful, Mike, you don't want to overwhelm him.

Michael Well, that's more like it. Right, that means ... (*He makes swift mental calculations*) Barnaby, can I have a word with you?

Barnaby Sure, Michael.

Barnaby and Michael walk aside, talking together

Lynne What's this, then? "Letting I dare not wait upon I would"?

Frank Not at all.

Lynne So why the volte-face?

Frank It's not what you think. It's just—well, did you know he rang me at work today three times, after I'd broken the news? Pleading with me.

Lynne He did murmur something about it.

Frank Well, in the end, I thought to myself, hold on. It's our own standards we've been judging him by, not his. Who are we to decide his priorities for him? This play is the most important thing in his life at the moment.

Lynne That's pretty brutal.
Frank Isn't it true?
Lynne But I'm sure if he knew . . .
Frank Well, he's not going to know, is he? We're going to be brave little martyrs. It'll probably help our performances.

Eric enters

Lynne Oh, it's good to have you back, Frank.
Frank Hey, what's got into Barnaby?

Barnaby is walking slowly away from Michael, looking miserable. Sally goes up to him and puts her arm round his shoulder. Michael looks at his script

Lynne I don't know. I've never seen him like——
Michael Right. We can't do the scene we're supposed to, because we haven't got Terry. Or Joe. Or Brian. But we can finally make a start on something—Act Three, Scene Two, it'll have to be. But I'm getting pretty pissed off with the way you've all been turning up late for rehearsal. It's bad enough having people missing altogether, without everyone else just waltzing in when they feel like it. Now, look, I've said this before, it's a commitment. We're not doing it for fun, you know, it's a serious business. If you can't have your dinner and still get here on time, you miss your dinner. Is that understood?

Murmurs of grudging assent

OK. Well, we've had a slice of good luck—three quite good men from St Luke's Players have agreed to join the cast for this show, which means I've been able to switch a few parts round and generally strengthen the cast. It doesn't affect . . . (*looking round*) anybody here . . . apart from Barnaby. Oh, if you wouldn't mind, Barnaby, could you still read in the Servant's part tonight?
Barnaby Sure, Michael.
Lynne Mike!
Frank Don't make it worse, Lynne.
Lynne (*approaching Barnaby*) Barnaby . . . oh, I'm so sorry.
Barnaby It's all right, Lynne. I am better selling programmes, aren't I?
Lynne Is that what he told you?
Michael OK. Three: Two. Macbeth and Lady Macbeth.

Frank crosses himself, twice

Now, do you remember what I was saying the other night? (*His voice gradually takes on a different quality; softer, more authoritative*) This is the scene where it really starts to notice. They're losing touch with each other. For the first time in their marriage, he's starting to have secrets from her. Now, they may have had their rows in the past, and their little disagreements, all that, but this is something new. "Be innocent of the knowledge, dearest chuck." That's the start of a gradual moving away—something he can't help—he's taking the weight of the murder and all that it entails on to his own shoulders—out of kindness, ironically—but it means she's being excluded from his world. Now, I don't want it obvious, or too poignant; just let that aspect of it be there under the surface. OK?

Lynne is about to speak. Frank stops her. Barnaby positions himself for the scene

Not there, Barnaby. Downstage right.

Barnaby moves

OK, Lynne, from up left.

They start rehearsing the scene

Lynne   Is Banquo gone from court?
Barnaby Ay, madam, but returns again tonight.
Lynne   Say to the king, I would attend his leisure
             For a few words.
Barnaby Madam, I will.

He wanders off the stage. Michael is looking down at his script. Lynne fixes him with her eyes

Lynne   Nought's had, all's spent
             Where our desire is got without content.

The lights begin to fade to black-out

             'Tis safer to be that which we destroy
             Than by destruction dwell in doubtful joy.

Black-out. A babble, as of a jumble sale. The lights go up on the church hall—a jumble sale. The only people we see are Alan and Fiona, together behind a table piled high with cheap and tatty books

Alan Books, lovely books! Masterpieces o' world literature at knockdown prices!

Fiona Masterpieces of world literature, that's a good one. Five hundred Mills and Boons, a *Treasure Island* with its cover missing, and two years of National Geographic.

Alan You should see the things we turned down.

Fiona Dunno why there's always a book stall at jumble sales. No one ever buys anything.

Alan It's for blokes like me to stand behind. I'm no good with clothes—dunno what to charge for 'em. With books you just go by 'ow thick they are. Or 'ow thick the customer is.

Fiona (*laughing*) But you shouldn't have charged that little old lady fifty pence for the Dennis Wheatley. It wasn't worth half that.

Alan It was, considerin' I just seen 'er stuff three skirts in 'er bag without payin' for 'em. Swings an' roundabouts, this game.

Fiona You can't judge a book by its cover, can you?

Alan Well, she certainly couldn't—that Dennis Wheatley 'ad its last three pages missin'.

Fiona laughs

Sally comes in

Sally You want your float toppin' up?
Fiona No, thanks, we've hardly sold a thing.
Sally Goin' well on the whole. Loads o' money taken at the door.
Alan Charge 'em double to get out, that's what I say.
Sally Only wish some o' these people'd come an' see us when we're puttin' on a play.
Alan Should call ourselves the Shellsfoot Jumble Sale Society. That's where the big money is.
Sally One woman asked me what play we was doin' next. I said I couldn't tell her the name but it was Scottish. Oh, she got quite excited, said her husband was Scottish, an' was there any bagpipe music in it?
Alan That's an idea.
Fiona We should have a band come on in the interval, like the Cup Final.
Alan Yeah.
Sally Pity the posters weren't ready for today.
Fiona Oh, don't you start. Mike was livid. He's been a real pig over publicity. I don't know why I took it on.
Sally Oh, we always give it to the new people.
Fiona I keep telling him, on my budget you can't have two colours on the poster. Red and black, he says, it must be red and black. And it wasn't my fault we missed the posting dates for the council.
Sally What, the official notice boards, all round the town?
Fiona Yeah. They had to be in by yesterday. Now they won't get put up till the twenty-third.
Sally That's the day after we close.
Fiona I said it was the best we could do. He got really nasty and told me to phone the mayor.
Alan Most o' these officials can be squared. Probably only take you a couple o' nights.

Alan turns away. Sally mouths to Fiona: "Do you want me to relieve you?" Fiona mouths "no" and shakes her head. Sally gestures questioningly at Alan, Fiona indicates she's happy with him. Sally looks surprised and pleased; Fiona looks smug. Alan by this time is watching

Don't tell me—"Gone with the Wind".

Fiona turns away, embarrassed

Sally An' where is Mr Director today, may I ask?
Alan 'E's at 'ome, I think. Reblockin' a couple of scenes.
Sally Typical. Expects everyone else to slave away to raise money for his big spectacular, but he won't dirty his hands to join in. Even snapped at me at rehearsal the other night when I was tryin' to sell raffle tickets.
Fiona We *were* on stage, Sal.
Sally Yeah, well. Oh, I see Mr and Mrs Scottish are together as usual. On shoes.
Alan Looks like it.

Sally They're inseparable these days. I'm sure there's somethin' goin' on. Some bloke was tryin' on a boot just now, and they both 'ad their 'and in it.

Alan Sure sign.

Sally I've always *thought* Lynne could do better if she wanted, but people say Mike's quite nice when you get to know 'im. Mind you, they haven't said that lately.

Fiona I thought Frank was supposed to be Michael's friend.

Alan That's what Banquo thought.

Sally Who?

Fiona Hey, look, Sal, there's an old geezer walkin' off with your coat!

Sally (*turning and gasping*) Bold as brass!—Hey, you—'scuse me!—That's not for sale ...

She runs off

Fiona Poor old Sal, she does go through it.

They laugh

Alan Well, we're wastin' our time 'ere. What you say to a quick five minutes under the table?

Fiona (*looking*) There's no room, it's a trestle.

Alan Ah, well. (*Shouting*) Books, lovely books!

Fiona Masterpieces of world literature at knockdown prices ...

Black-out. Fade jumble sale noise; fade up a morning radio programme— traffic news. Fade when scene established. The lights go up on Lynne's and Michael's lounge. The stage is empty

Michael enters sleepily in his trousers, pyjama jacket and bare feet, carrying a cup of tea, shirt, jacket, tie, socks and shoes. He sits down, and begins with great difficulty to put on the socks

Lynne (*off; surprised*) Oh! Mike?

Michael Mmm?

Lynne (*off*) Where are you?

Michael Mmm. (*He gives up with the socks, and sits staring out front*)

Lynne comes in

Lynne Oh, you got up! I thought I was going to have to pour cold water over you.

Michael Mmm.

Lynne Well, then. Happy anniversary. (*She kisses him and gives him a small parcel*)

Michael Wha—— is it?

Lynne Sure is. Thursday November the sixth. M minus twelve, in your language. Don't worry, you needn't tell me you'd forgotten. You don't have to be directing a play to forget our wedding anniversary.

Michael I am sorry, love. I'll get you something ...

Lynne No, you won't, it's the thought that counts. Anyway, you haven't called a rehearsal tonight, that's my present. It'll be nice having you to myself for a change.

Michael (*starting to get dressed*) Why haven't I called a rehearsal? I was trying to figure that out.

Lynne Well, as a matter of fact you did write one in your schedule, but I crossed it out and wrote "KEEP FREE" in your handwriting. I thought that was the safest way.

Michael You're getting devious.

Lynne Come on, you'll be late for work again.

Michael Oh, God, don't say that.

Lynne If you will rehearse till all hours ... I've begun to wish we had a normal church hall like other groups, with a crotchety caretaker who kicks us out at ten o'clock sharp ...

A ring at the doorbell

Oh, no, who's this?

She goes out

(*Off*) If it's Alan, I'll tell him you've left. I'm not having you rabbiting on all morning——

A door opens off-stage

Oh, hello!

Geraldine (*off*) Good-morning, my dear.

Michael looks alarmed, and starts looking around for a weapon

So sorry to call so early, but I wanted to catch dear Michael before he went to work. I'd so hate to inconvenience him in the office again.

Lynne (*off*) He's just leaving, actually——

Geraldine (*off*) I shan't keep him a minute.

Lynne (*off*) In there ...

Door closes, off. Geraldine enters, followed by Lynne

Michael Hello, Geraldine.

Geraldine Oh, good, you remembered my name.

Lynne Won't you sit down?

Geraldine No, thank you.

Michael Excuse my ... er ...

Geraldine I thought it was my duty to warn you. You'll be hearing from the vicar this evening.

Michael Really? Why?

Geraldine Poor Simon's a little concerned. It's been brought to his attention that there are certain elements in The Scottish Play that really aren't suitable for his church hall.

Lynne Such as what?

Geraldine Such as the witches, and the incantations, and the black magic. He's very worried about it.

Michael They're absolutely vital to the play—especially to this production.

I couldn't cut any of it without throwing the whole thing off balance.
Geraldine That's exactly what I said to him. "Simon," I said, "if those parts
are removed, you might just as well remove the whole production."

They stare at her

Michael You didn't really say that.
Geraldine Perhaps you didn't expect me to be so strong in your defence. But
Simon did understand, you know. He is quite a devotee of the Drama.
Michael So what's he going to do?
Geraldine He's banning it, Michael. Such a pity, such a shame. The
Thespians' first venture into Shakespeare—how sad it hasn't worked out
in the end. But, still—The Scottish Play—well, we make our own luck,
don't we?
Michael Now just a minute——
Geraldine How long have you got, now? Twelve days? Oh, that's ample.
Quite long enough for two such talented young people to mount a little
one-acter. Or perhaps you could give a series of lectures on how Amateur
Dramatic Societies should be run?
Lynne Geraldine——
Geraldine Anyway, I must dash now. I just wanted to be the first to tell you.
Lynne You bloody old cow!
Geraldine I may be a lot of things, Lynne, but at least I'm not married to
that!

She goes out

Stunned silence

Lynne Darling—— (*She puts her hand on his shoulder*)
Michael Don't. I'm trying to think.
Lynne Mike, I'm so sorry. I never thought anybody could be so vindictive.
Not even her. God, she was enjoying it, wasn't she?
Michael What's the vicar's number? Have we got it?
Lynne Yes, it's in the book, under "v".

*Michael gets up and scans the pages of an address book. He finds the number
and starts dialling*

What are you going to do?
Michael How the hell do I know? (*He makes a mistake*) Oh, shit, I've—just
shut up, will you?
Lynne Sure, Mike. Can't I do anything?
Michael Yes, you can leave me alone. Stop hovering over me. Go and . . . go
to work.
Lynne OK, Mike. Whatever you want.

He turns back to the phone

She is about to go and kiss him goodbye, but thinks better of it, and goes

*The lights fade on Michael dialling again. In the Black-out, the ringing tone is
heard, and after a few seconds a different ringing tone takes over. Typing is*

heard in the background. The lights go up on Michael's desk at Cooper & Dye.
He is wearing his pyjama jacket, suit and no tie. Jackie, at her desk, can be
seen dimly in the background. The ringing tone ends

Frank is suddenly lit at another part of the stage. He has just picked up his
own phone

Frank Hello?
Michael Oh, bloody marvellous, at long last! Where've you been, then,
guzzling the communion wine, or pocketing the collection?
Frank Who is that?
Michael Who's that?
Frank Michael?
Michael Frank! Oh, God, what'm I doing—I've been trying to phone the
vicar all morning, then I gave up and phoned you instead.
Frank What's up? You at work?
Michael Yes—Les is out all morning, thank God. Haven't you heard?
Frank I don't think I can have. What?
Michael Geraldine's got the vicar to ban us.
Frank Good Lord! . . . What, the whole show?
Michael Yep. She popped in this morning to break the news. Gloating with
sympathy.
Frank Oh, Michael, I am sorry. So—what're you going to do?
Michael Well, my first job's to try and talk him out of it, but I don't hold
out much hope of that.
Frank Not if your opening gambit's anything to go by. Anyway, he's not
likely to turn against Geraldine. She's twisted him so far round her little
finger he doesn't know his arse from his elbow.
Michael I tried phoning Alan, see if he's got any bright ideas, but his
number's unobtainable.
Frank Thank God most of the bills haven't been paid yet.
Michael What?
Frank The drapes, for instance. We can return them without losing
anything——
Michael Is that all you can think about? Money?
Frank Of course not, but——
Michael I don't care a damn about the bills. We're in business to put on
plays, not to avoid spending money. I'll do the show over Geraldine's
dead body. And the vicar's, if necessary.
Frank Don't be silly, Michael. He's got every right to do what he likes with
his own church hall.
Michael I can get that kind of talk from my wife, thank you very much. If
you've nothing constructive to——
Frank No, Michael, no. If there's anything I can do, just call me.

The receivers are replaced; Frank's light goes out

A phone rings again; light up on Jackie

Michael (*answering his phone*) Yes?

Jackie Someone called Alan?
Michael Yeah, yeah.

Jackie's light goes off

A light comes up on Alan, with a phone

Alan, where've you been? I've been trying to ring you. Have you heard——
Alan Yeah, I met your missis in town. Bad luck, boss.
Michael Spare me the sympathy.
Alan Right, then. I've got a list of all the church 'alls, schools an' clubs in town. There's thirty-eight of 'em. I can go round ten, 'cos they're not too far to walk. You wanna ring the other twenty-eight, if I give you the numbers?
Michael (*impressed*) Alan, I——
Alan I would, only my phone's bin cut off.
Michael Where are you, then?
Alan Reference library. Spend a lot o' time 'ere. I know the girl on the desk, but I don't know 'er well enough for twenty-eight calls. (*He looks off-stage*) Do I, pet? She says no, I don't.
Michael Alan, you're magnificent.
Alan Get a pencil, then. Must be some place in this town where you can 'old black rites ...

Black-out; then a light comes up on Jackie

Jackie (*on the phone*) Oh, good-mornin'. I'm phonin' on be'alf of the Shellsfoot Thepsians. They're doin' this play, see, an'——

The lights switch to Michael

Michael ... the only trouble is, our usual hall isn't available. (*Pause*) Surely in the interests of education ... (*Pause*) Well, for God's sake, don't you teach Shakespeare at your school? (*Pause*) Oh, I'm sorry, I ... I thought it was a convent *school*. ... Yes. ... Yes. ... Sorry, er ... madam ...

The lights switch to Jackie

Jackie ... then the vicar says no they can't because it's full o' black magic an' evil an' fings, an' ... 'ello?

The lights switch to Michael

Michael ... no, it has to be that week, or at worst the week after. Can't the W.I. be put off? ... No, well, thanks anyway. (*He slams the phone down*) God.

The phone rings. He picks it up

Yeah?

A light comes up on Jackie

Jackie Alan for you, Mike.
Michael Oh, right.

A light comes up on Alan, as the light goes off Jackie

Hi, Alan. Any luck?

Alan Not a lot. Most places are booked up at least one night that week.

Michael I wonder if any other towns in the area——

Alan Only place free's the bleedin' Town Hall.

Michael What?

Alan Big ballroom, you know it? They've just 'ad it repainted, and it was ready quicker than they thought, so there's no bookin's for the next three weeks.

Michael But——

Alan Shame, there's a stage an' dressin'-rooms an' everything.

Michael So why not?

Alan Well, I checked. It's three 'undred quid just to 'ire it for a week.

Michael Three hundred? (*Pause*) That's OK.

Alan But the lightin' there's bleedin' basic—we'd 'ave to get more lanterns an' spots——

Michael How much?

Alan Buildin' out the stage—rehearsal time—all told, say six 'undred?

Michael Alan, quick. Get back there and tell them we'll have it. Every evening from tomorrow to the last night of the show.

Alan But, boss——

Michael Seven-thirty till midnight, and all day Saturday and Sunday. We'll build the set and rig the lights after rehearsal and Saturday morning.

Alan They said somethin' about a deposit—hundred quid, I think.

Michael You can get that from Sally.

Alan No way, boss. No more cash from the group; she's told me that, only what's bin agreed.

Michael Oh, God! . . . Look, *I* can pay the money for the time being——

Alan You won't get it back.

Michael Alan, don't *you* start being obstructive. Can you pay from your own money for now?

Alan I ain't even got a cheque book.

A light suddenly comes up on Dye. He is standing in reception, next to Jackie, and is using Jackie's phone

Dye Never mind, Mikey. Why don't you just pop down to the Town Hall an' pay them yeself?

Alan Who's that?

Michael Er . . . hello, Les. I'm . . . er . . . can I just explain . . .

Dye No need to, Mikey. I've 'eard most of this; it's been quite instructive. Now, six hundred pounds—that's as near as makes no difference to one month's salary, isn't it? Well, I always pay a month in advance to anyone leavin' my employ.

Michael What . . . what are you talking about?

Alan I'll be off then, shall I?

Dye I think you've had sufficient warning, Mikey, and I seem to recall a memo I sent you on the subject last week—habitual lateness, short hours, mind not fully on the job—not half on it, if you ask me—excessive use of company phones for private calls—an' today, from what I gather, usin' the offices of Cooper and Dye as some sort of theatrical agency.

Michael Please, Les, I promise——

Dye There's myriads out there who'd snap up your job. Now, hadn't you better get down to that Town Hall before Bernard Delfont puts in his bid?

He replaces his receiver, and his light goes out. Pause

Michael Alan, are you still there?

Alan Just about.

Michael I'll see you at the Town Hall in ... twenty minutes. I'll pop in the building society, it's on the way.

Alan Right, boss.

Alan puts down his phone, and his light goes out. Michael leans forward, thinking, as his light gradually fades to Black-out

Michael God, the Town Hall! It must seat ... five hundred? ... oh, at least. We'll need more publicity ... a couple of hundred more posters at least ... and all the ones we've put up already'll have to come down. I wonder what the sight-lines are like? Have to check that; and the acoustics ...

Black-out. The sound of wind, as at the start of the play; then lights up gradually on Michael's and Lynne's lounge. Lynne is on the phone

Lynne Uh, huh? ... Right, then. ... Yes. ... I don't know, I really don't, I ... Oh, God, that sounds like him. ... Yeah. ... OK, love, speak to you soon ... *(She puts the phone down)*

Michael comes in. He is a little tipsy, euphoric and dishevelled

Michael Hello, Lynne?

Lynne Hello.

Michael Oh, you're there. God, is it ten o'clock? ... Lynne, you'll never believe my luck.

Lynne Yes, I will. I've just been talking to Frank.

Michael Frank?

Lynne You know, Macbeth. He ... em ... rang me. To tell me what was going on, in case I was worried about you.

Michael Yeah, I got him to come over to the Town Hall, to test his voice on the acoustics. Has he told you the whole story?

Lynne I expect so.

Michael I've been there with Alan for hours, just working everything out——

Lynne And then you went to the pub.

Michael Yeah, briefly. Celebrate. *(He sits, yawning)* Anyway, I'm home now.

Lynne You're home now. And I suppose you want something to eat.

Michael Well, I wouldn't say no.

Lynne God, that's awfully big of you, Mike. Any particular preference, or shall I just dish up the special dinner I made for our anniversary?

Pause

Michael Oh, God.

Lynne Wives are useful things, aren't they? Specially to high-powered theatre directors. They'll support you. They're loyal. Some of them can act quite well and you can give them parts in your play; even if they don't really want them. Then when you feel like kicking everyone around, and the actors complain and threaten to resign, you can always count on your wife to defend you, and tell them how much pressure you're under, and it's all for the good of the show. Maybe something dreadful happens— she'll offer to help, and better than that, she's bright enough to understand when you boot her out of the way because you're upset. (*Getting worked up*) And best of all, when you come home plastered in the middle of the night, the dear little woman won't complain. Not even when it's her bloody wedding anniversary——

Michael (*getting up and going to her*) Lynne—please——

Lynne Don't touch me. Get off.

Michael I'm sorry . . .

Lynne No, you're not. You're not sorry. You just want me to shut up so you can think about your precious *Macbeth*.

Michael I'd no idea you felt like this. I thought . . . I thought things were getting better.

Lynne What, all by themselves?

Michael I don't know, I——

Lynne It might have looked that way to you, because I've been making an effort. P'raps if *you'd* made an effort too, things might actually have *got* better.

Michael I'm a bit obtuse, I know——

Lynne Did you know I was having an affair with Frank?

Michael What?

Lynne I hadn't meant to tell you, but I think you deserve it.

Michael With Frank?

Lynne Macbeth and Lady Macbeth. Cosy, isn't it?

Michael When did you——

Lynne Oh, long before you cast us together. We *had* decided to put a stop to it. For your sake, partly—God knows why. That's why I didn't want the part. That's why Frank had to pretend that he'd——

Michael Oh, Lynne. (*He sits*)

Lynne And I suppose you were going to tell me some time that you'd been sacked from Cooper and Dye?

Michael I——

Lynne Jackie phoned to ask what she should do with the personal effects you'd left in your desk. Oh, Mike, it wouldn't have been so bad if you'd been too ashamed to tell me. But it's quite obvious you just couldn't care less!

Michael Of course I——

Lynne And where's all this extra money coming from? Have you been robbing the firm? I wouldn't put anything past you.

Michael No, I went to the building society.

Pause

Lynne I see. So you haven't been robbing the firm. You've been robbing us.
Michael Lynne, I promise you. As soon as the play's over——
Lynne Shut up! I don't want to hear you. I just want to tell you something.
I've had enough, and I'm getting out.
Michael Lynne!
Lynne Don't worry, I'm not pulling out of the cast. Not at this stage, I'm
not that mean. (*Calmer*) I'm just leaving *you*, Michael. It's best for both of
us, at least for the next few weeks. You need to be on your own, now. I'm
just one of your actresses—you don't want me around when I've not been
called. And I'm afraid I simply can't put up with it any longer. I'll go
round to Mum's—I rang her tonight and told her to expect me.
Michael (*at sea*) Lynne . . . I love you . . .
Lynne (*quietly*) Oh. Yes, I expect you do. But it's not really relevant now.

The Lights fade on them, staring at each other

*Frank and Eric come in, in shadow, on one side of Michael, and Lynne goes
out. We are on the Town Hall stage at a rehearsal; Daisy and Alan are also
there, watching; but at first no one is lit*

Frank I have almost forgot the taste of fears:
The time has been, my senses would have cooled
To hear a night shriek, and my fell of hair
Would at a dismal treatise rouse and stir
As life were in't. I have supped full of horrors.
Direness, familiar to my slaughterous thoughts
Cannot once stir me.

*A light comes up on Michael's head as Eric (Seton) is seen in shadow coming
downstage. Michael speaks intensely, almost feverishly*

Michael Seton returns, but he can't face Macbeth with the news he has to
tell him. He walks downstage, slowly coming level with his master,
praying that something will happen to prevent him having to break the
news. He stops. They both stand there a second, two seconds. Then,
unsuspecting, Macbeth turns his head.
Frank (*still in shadow*) Wherefore was that cry?
Eric (*still in shadow*) The queen, my lord, is dead.
Michael Pause. Nothing. Look at him. Not upset, not unbelieving, just
absorbing the words, just staring into his eyes. Then . . . let the waves
come crashing over you.

The lights come up very slowly

Let go of your acting, let go your technique. There's no such person as
Shakespeare, you're not a character in a play. You're just a man, a man
whose wife has died.
Frank (*speaking the verse quite well, but without any great feeling*)

She should have died hereafter.
There would have been a time for such a word.
Tomorrow and tomorrow and——

Michael No, no, no. It still won't do. It sounds as if your pet budgie had died.

Frank Give me a chance to work it up——

Michael No, it's got to come straight away. If you're not feeling it in the first place, you'll never convince the audience. It's a string of clichés, this, the whole bloody speech is in the Penguin Book of Quotations. Your only chance is to make them think they've never heard it before, that you're making it up on the spur of the moment.

Frank I *will* get it, I know I'm nearly there——

Michael You won't until you stop trying. Look, I could hear the calculations as you were choosing how to stress the words, and remembering what you'd been intending to do with it. That won't help.

Frank Let's try it later, when everyone's gone home.

Michael No! We'll try it now, with everyone watching. There'll be an audience watching in three days' time, you know. And that's all the time we've got; we have to get it right now.

Frank turns away, deep in thought

Don't act it, *be* it. This scene above all. It's a shattering blow, the biggest you could give to a man. Think about it, Frank, think, relate to it . . . your wife has died. Think . . . (*A sudden thought*) Imagine it's Lynne, Frank. Imagine it's her.

Frank swings round and glares at him

Frank You . . . bastard.

Michael (*almost visibly channelling Frank's emotion*) Yeah, I know. But think it.

Pause; then Frank does the speech as Michael directed; very movingly

Frank She should have died hereafter.
There would have been a time for such a word.
Tomorrow and tomorrow and tomorrow
Creeps in this petty pace from day to day
To the last syllable of recorded time,
And all our yesterdays have lighted fools
The way to dusty death. Out, out, brief candle!
Life's but a walking shadow, a poor player
That struts and frets his hour upon the stage
And then is heard no more: it is a tale
Told by an idiot, full of sound and fury,
Signifying nothing.

Pause, then Daisy, Eric and Alan all clap

Michael (*triumphant*) Well, come on! Enter a messenger—where's the bloody messenger?

Black-out. We hear, after a pause, the lines that follow from Sally

When the lights go up, we are in the women's dressing room at the Town Hall, just before the first performance of "Macbeth". Lynne is sitting quietly in a corner; Sally pacing and reciting her lines without expression; Fiona reading; Mary changing

Sally (*before lights up*)   A sailor's wife had chestnuts in her lap
And munched and munched and munched. "Give me," quoth I.

The lights come slowly up

"Aroint thee, witch!" the rump-fed ronyon cries.
Her husband's to Aleppo——
Fiona If you don't know it now, Sal, you'll never know it.
Sally Ooh, don't say that!
Fiona Just try and keep your mind clear. Don't clutter it up, you'll get tense.
Sally I can only act when I'm tense!

Alan comes in

Alan Daisy says fifteen minutes.
Sally Oh, God!
Fiona You should knock, love.
Alan What, an' give you all a chance to cover yourselves up?
Sally (*nostalgically*) In the church 'all we was all in together.
Alan Wicked places, church 'alls.
Mary Ooh, I got to go to the loo again ...

She runs out

Sally That's five times.
Fiona Shouldn't you be in your lighting-box?
Alan I've checked it all out. Just thought I'd come an' say 'ello.
Sally Is there any sign of 'is majesty yet?
Alan No. Nobody's seen 'im.
Fiona Funny.
Sally I 'ope 'e's all right.
Fiona Maybe he got the date wrong.
Sally Well, we all got cards from 'im, anyway.
Alan Did yer? Good luck cards?
Fiona I think mine said good luck at the bottom, after all the notes on the dress rehearsal.
Sally He gave me thirty-seven notes. I counted 'em before I tore it up.
Fiona You're all right, Sal, you don't need notes. He's nit-picking now, he said himself last night it was getting to be quite good.
Sally Comin' from 'im, that's like a Nobel Prize. Mean old——

She puts her hand to her mouth. Everyone looks at Lynne, who is still sitting quietly in her corner. Alan mouths: "She OK?" Sally shrugs

Alan Right, better go or you'll all be in darkness. Break all yer legs, won't you?—Oh, this came for you.

He hands an envelope to Fiona and goes

Sally Notes from the bloody lightin'-box, now, is it?

Fiona I expect it's a good luck card, bless him. (*She opens it and reads it*) Oh, it's a kitten. He's quite soft, you know, underneath.

Sally Oh, yes.

Fiona "To the most bewitching witch on the whole blasted heath. Double double toil and trouble, break a leg and give me a cuddle. Love and kisses, lighting person." Aaah.

Sally Aaah.

Fiona "PS. Will you marry me?" What?

She stares speechless at Sally, then they hug

Fiona runs out

Sally Bless 'er, she's a sweet kid. (*Pause*) I think they're just right for each other, don't you? (*Pause*) You asleep, Lynne?

Lynne Sorry, I was miles away. I sort of withdraw into myself when I'm in a play.

Sally Yeah, everyone's different. I get noisier. If possible! Nervous?

Lynne A little. It's all come rather suddenly, I haven't had time to get nervous.

Sally You bin through a lot these last few weeks, an't you?

Lynne You could say that.

Sally Don't get us wrong, what we were sayin' about Mike. 'E's probably a very good director an' everything, an' 'e's done wonders with this show, 'e's just not really ... well, right for us. You know? I mean, the Thespians have always had real fun before, but ... 'e's sort of stopped all that.

Lynne Yes, I know. It's a pity that his great ambition in life turned out to be something that had to involve other people.

Sally Yeah.

Lynne You know who I bumped into the other day? Poor Barnaby's mother.

Sally Oh, Lord.

Lynne They've only just wormed it out of Barnaby why he's been so down the last few weeks. He hadn't even told them till last Saturday that he'd lost the part. She was saying Michael had no right to do it. It was giving candy to a baby and then snatching it away again.

Sally Well, 'e's not a normal kid, is he? I remember 'im sayin', 'is parents got 'im to join the Thespians to keep 'im out of the 'ouse, away from his mum's apron-strings. He used to tell me how happy he was now he'd got all of us for friends.

Lynne I didn't mention it to her ... but it occurred to me as she was talking that in a strange sort of way Mike's position isn't a whole lot different from Barnaby's. They've both been given a taste of something special, something they'd been yearning for ... and suddenly the dream's over.

Well, at least Barnaby's got his programmes to sell. And maybe when he
gets his confidence back he'll land a part in some play with a more ...
sympathetic director. Whereas Mike ...
Sally Yeah. Well, anyway, we don't want 'im directin' us again. The
committee decided that the other night.
Lynne Was Geraldine there?
Sally No. She resigned, didn't you know? And Arnold, of course. I daresay
they'll be back as soon as this is over.
Lynne Yes.
Sally You 'eard from Mike at all today?
Lynne Well, I got notes, the same as everyone else. I can't really expect
special treatment, can I?
Sally (*sitting down*) You've bin a bit in limbo, 'aven't you? Stayin' with yer
mum, an' that. Have yer still not made yer mind up, what yer gonna do?
Lynne Yes. Yes, I think I have.

Fiona enters

Sally Oh, Fiona! Did you catch 'im?
Fiona No, he'd gone.
Sally What're you gonna say?
Fiona What do you think?
Sally Ohh! (*She hugs her again*)

Mary enters

Fiona Oh, Daisy says ten minutes.

Mary rushes out again

Sally Shit!
Fiona And this is for you, Lynne. (*She gives her a red rose*)
Lynne From ... ?
Fiona From Frank, of course.
Lynne Bless him. (*She smells it*)
Sally (*rattling it off*) "But in a sieve I'll thither sail and like a rat without a
tail I'll do and I'll do and I'll do ..."

*The lights fade to black-out as Sally speaks. Now we hear, gradually growing,
the sound of the audience arriving—as heard from the lighting box. Alan is
heard approaching, whistling. He switches on a light: we are in the lighting
box, and Michael is sitting there*

Alan Oh! God, you shouldn't do that, boss. I nearly fell out o' the box.
Michael Sorry, I thought I'd watch from up here, at least to start with. I'm
not in the way, am I?
Alan No, not if you shove over a bit.

Michael does; Alan sits

Tell yer what, if yer wanna be useful, you can stick them cans on yer 'ead
an' tell me if Daisy's sayin' anything.
Michael (*doing so*) All quiet at present.

Alan She just told me ten minutes.

Michael Ten minutes.

Alan Not bad 'ouse for first night?

Michael Not bad at all.

Alan I reckon that sob story in the paper about losin' the church 'all must 'ave 'elped.

Michael Any crisis is good publicity.

Alan The gang was wonderin' where you were.

Michael I didn't see much point in hanging around backstage, making them nervous. I left them all one or two notes.

Alan Yeah, they said. Sal's just started volume two of 'ers—I'm waitin' for the film.

Michael How's Lynne, OK?

Alan Yeah.

Michael Good.

Alan You all right, boss? You look tired.

Michael Tired, unkempt and generally gone to the dogs. You should see the state of the house! Well, at least I'm past being nervous.

Alan Glad somebody is.

Michael You nervous?

Alan You're not the only bloke thinks this show's important, you know.

Michael I know, Alan, you've been great—all the way through.

Alan I wouldn't 'ave done it if I 'adn't wanted to.

Michael But you've worked harder than anyone else. Apart from me, of course.

Alan Yeah, well, I could afford to, couldn't I?

Michael Mmm?

Alan Sorry, forget I said that.

Michael Don't be silly. What do you mean?

Alan Well ... I've no responsibilities, 'ave I? No job, yet. No wife ... Nothin' else to do. It's even bin an' 'elp, you know—my new job, I said at the interview I'd got experience doin' lightin' an' sets—showed 'em the model an' that. I reckon it was that swung me the job.

Michael Terrific.

Alan An' ... you know Fiona? Second witch?

Michael Yes.

Alan Well, then.

Michael Aha! (*He laughs*) I'm glad to hear the play's been of use to somebody. Well, our roles are reversed now, Alan.

Alan That's why I shouldn't have——

Michael Don't worry. I'll find another job, some time. And I expect ... I suppose ... Lynne will ... well, I can't see her going to Frank, not when it comes to it ... Anyway, I'm not looking beyond the end of this week.

Alan No.

Michael God, look at all those people!

Alan Gets the old adrenalin goin', eh?

Michael Yeah ... I wonder how many of them will really appreciate it? I mean, even appreciate half of what we're trying to put across?

Alan Rough estimate—none of 'em?

Michael We'll get two crits, one in the *Herald* and one in the *Gazette*. Some punning cliché in the headline, two paragraphs telling the story of the play, and then a list of who played what part—with a special mention for the porter because he's the only bit of humour in an otherwise dark and gloomy evening.

Alan That bother you?

Michael Just as long as it works. We'll know.

Alan It will, boss. It's a bloody good show. Everyone says so, even the ones who've complained.

Michael When I first thought of doing it, you know what I felt? I felt, now, at last, I have a chance of doing something I really want to do. Something I think I've got a talent for—a way of fulfilling myself at last. And in a sense it was *because* I hated my job, and *because* things weren't going too well at home. I thought I could prove something to the world. Or at least to ... those about me.

Alan You've proved it to yourself.

Michael Yeah. Tell me, Alan ... do you have any time for all these superstitions about *Macbeth*?

Suddenly, in a different part of the stage, a light goes up on Lynne. She is sitting in the Stage Manager's seat in the wings, with the cans on her head

Lynne Hello?

Michael Oh ... Daisy's calling.

Alan Switch the mike on—there. Hey, can you sound like me?

Michael I'll try. (*He switches on the mike*) 'Ello, Daisy?

Lynne It's Lynne, actually, Alan. Daisy says we're just about to go up. One minute.

Michael Er ... right.

Lynne I've got a message from Fiona. She says she can't talk now 'cos she's about to go on, but she says yes she will.

Michael Will what?

Lynne (*laughing*) Come off it, Alan! Congratulations, anyway. And ... er ... I suppose you wouldn't consider the idea of a double celebration after the show? You see, Frank and I have arrived at a little decision—rather like yours.

Michael (*taking the cans off and passing them; quietly*) It's for you, Alan. (*His head sinks into his hands*)

Alan Oh, right ... (*He puts on the cans*) 'Ello?

Lynne What's going on?

Alan Alan 'ere.

Lynne Well, who was that?

Alan Oh ... my assistant. Goin' up in the world.

Daisy enters, next to Lynne

Lynne Look, we're just about to start. Tell him to pass on the message, I'll see you afterwards. But it's congratulations all round, right?

Alan Oh! ... Great ... er ... break a leg, then.

Lynne takes off the cans and gives them to Daisy, who takes her seat

Lynne exits

Sorry, boss.

Daisy Stand by LX Cue One. LX Cue One go.

Alan moves a slide on the board; the lights go down, gradually, and the audience's talking subsides

Alan You OK? . . . Michael?

Michael Shh—listen. That's right: the way the talking subsides, everyone's attentive in the dark, waiting for something to fill the space in front of them.

The Lights fade to Black-out, except for the lighting box

Total blackout. Count three seconds . . . Thunder.

Thunder

Lightning.

A crash of thunder, together with a flash of lightning

Enter . . . three . . . witches . . .

The wind is heard, growing to a climax, then it stops suddenly and there is a simultaneous Black-out

FURNITURE AND PROPERTY LIST

ACT I

The stage of the church hall

On stage: Sofa with cushions
Chair
Coffee table

The dressing-room in the church hall

On stage: 2 chairs. *On them:* costumes
Table. *On it:* propped-up mirror, dry shampoo, make-up, comb, etc.

The offices of Cooper & Dye

On stage: Desk. *On it:* papers, telephone, pens, house lists, etc.
Chairs
Receptionist's desk. *On it:* typewriter, telephone, letters
Dye's desk. *On it:* papers, pens, etc.

Personal: **Michael:** wrist-watch (required throughout)

The bar in the church hall

On stage: 2 tables. *On one:* drinks for **Fiona** and **Sally**
Chairs
Orange juice for **Barnaby**

Off stage: Pint of beer (**Alan**)
Pint of beer (**Frank**)
Pint of beer, gin and tonic (**Michael**)

Michael's and Lynne's lounge

On stage: Sofa. *On it:* newspaper
Coffee table. *On it:* telephone, address book
Bowl of cereal for **Michael**

Off stage: Small table that glows red in the light (**Barnaby**)

The stage of the church hall

On stage: Table. *On it:* copy of *Macbeth*, papers, pen
Chairs
Copy of *Macbeth* for **Barnaby**

Michael's and Lynne's house

On stage: Lounge:
As before, plus:
Jug of coffee, mugs on coffee table

Copy of *Macbeth* for **Lynne**
Dining-room:
Table. *On it:* model of *Macbeth* set, chessmen, copy of *Macbeth*, papers, pens, etc.

The pub

On stage: Table
3 stools
Drinks for **Sally, Fiona** and **Barnaby**
Copy of *Macbeth* for **Barnaby**

Off stage: Model of *Macbeth* set (**Alan**)

The offices of Cooper & Dye

On stage: As before, plus;
Copy of *Macbeth* on **Michael**'s desk

Off stage: Telephone (**Frank**)

Personal: **Geraldine:** handbag with cheque book and pen

ACT II

The stage of the church hall

On stage: Chairs
Tables

Off stage: Script (**Lynne**)
Script, chalk, string (**Michael**)
Scripts (**Fiona, Sally**)
Script (**Mary**)
Script (**Frank**)
Script (**Eric**)
Script (**Barnaby**)

Personal: **Lynne:** wrist-watch

The jumble sale at the church hall

On stage: Table. *On it:* old books, magazines

Michael's and Lynne's lounge

On stage: As before

Off stage: Cup of tea, shirt, jacket, tie, shoes, socks (**Michael**)
Small parcel (**Lynne**)

The offices of Cooper & Dye

On stage: As before

Off stage: Telephone (**Frank**)
Telephone (**Alan**)

Michael's and Lynne's lounge

On stage: As before

The Town Hall stage

On stage: Nil

The dressing-room in the Town Hall

On stage; Table. *On it:* mirrors, make-up, etc.
              Chairs
              Costumes
              Script for **Fiona**

Off stage: Card in envelope (**Alan**)
              Red rose (**Fiona**)

Lighting box

On stage: 2 chairs
              Lighting board
              Headphones
              Microphone

Stage Manager's seat in the wings

On stage: Chair
              Headphones with microphone for **Lynne**

LIGHTING PLOT

Property fittings required: nil

Various simple interior settings

ACT I

Cue 15	**Eric:** "... have old turning the key ..."	(Page 17)
	Bring up lighting on church hall stage	
Cue 16	**Geraldine:** "Out, I say!"	(Page 20)
	Fade to black-out	
Cue 17	**Lynne:** "... our power to account?"	(Page 20)
	Light up on **Michael** *in dining-room*	
Cue 18	**Michael:** "... searing effect of the next line——"	(Page 20)
	Light up on **Lynne** *in lounge*	
Cue 19	**Lynne:** "... rubbing his hands."	(Page 23)
	Black-out, then bring up lighting on pub	
Cue 20	**Barnaby:** "... that do cling together——"	(Page 25)
	Fade slowly to black-out	
Cue 21	**Barnaby:** "... do swarm upon him ..."	(Page 25)
	Complete black-out, then bring up lighting on offices	
Cue 22	**Michael:** "God ... OK."	(Page 29)
	Bring up light on **Frank**	
Cue 23	**Michael** slams the phone down	(Page 30)
	Cut light on **Frank**	
Cue 24	**Dye** wheels round and stares at **Michael**	(Page 30)
	Black-out	

ACT II

To open:	Dim lighting on church hall	
Cue 25	**Michael** switches light on	(Page 31)
	Snap up lighting on church hall	
Cue 26	**Lynne:** "... is got without content."	(Page 34)
	Begin to fade lights	
Cue 27	**Lynne:** "... dwell in doubtful joy."	(Page 34)
	Black-out, then lights up on jumble sale	
Cue 28	**Fiona:** "... at knockdown prices ..."	(Page 36)
	Black-out, then bring up lighting on Lynne's and Michael's lounge	
Cue 29	**Lynne** goes; **Michael** dials again	(Page 38)
	Fade to black-out	
Cue 30	When ready	(Page 39)
	Bring up light on **Michael's** *desk at Cooper & Dye, with dim lighting on* **Jackie** *in background*	
Cue 31	Ringing tone ends	(Page 39)
	Snap up light on **Frank**	
Cue 32	**Frank** and **Michael** replace telephone receivers	(Page 39)
	Cut light on **Frank**	
Cue 33	Telephone rings	(Page 39)
	Increase light on **Jackie**	

Cue 34	**Michael:** "Yeah, yeah." *Cut light on* **Jackie,** *snap up light on* **Alan**	(Page 40)
Cue 35	**Alan:** "... 'old black rites ..." *Black-out; light up on* **Jackie**	(Page 40)
Cue 36	**Jackie:** "They're doin' this play, see, an'——" *Cut light on* **Jackie***; light up on* **Michael**	(Page 40)
Cue 37	**Michael:** "Yes. ... Sorry, er ... madam ..." *Cut light on* **Michael***; light up on* **Jackie**	(Page 40)
Cue 38	**Jackie:** "... an' fings, an' ... 'ello?" *Cut light on* **Jackie***; light up on* **Michael**	(Page 40)
Cue 39	**Michael** (*on the phone*): "Yeah?" *Light up on* **Jackie**	(Page 40)
Cue 40	**Michael:** "Oh, right." *Cut light on* **Jackie***; light up on* **Alan**	(Page 40)
Cue 41	**Alan:** "... got a cheque book." *Snap up light on* **Dye**	(Page 41)
Cue 42	**Dye** replaces his receiver *Cut light on* **Dye**	(Page 42)
Cue 43	**Alan** puts down his phone *Cut light on* **Alan** *and gradually fade light on* **Michael**	(Page 42)
Cue 44	**Michael:** "... and the acoustics ..." *Black-out*	(Page 42)
Cue 45	Sound of wind *Gradually bring up lights on Michael's and Lynne's lounge*	(Page 42)
Cue 46	**Lynne:** "... not really relevant now." *Fade lights*	(Page 44)
Cue 47	**Frank:** "Cannot once stir me." *Light up on* **Michael's** *head; shadowy lighting on* **Eric** *downstage*	(Page 44)
Cue 48	**Michael:** "... come crashing over you." *Bring up lights very slowly on Town Hall stage*	(Page 44)
Cue 49	**Michael:** "... the bloody messenger?" *Black-out*	(Page 45)
Cue 50	**Sally:** "'Give me,' quoth I." *Slowly bring up lights on dressing-room*	(Page 46)
Cue 51	**Sally:** "... I'll do and I'll do ..." *Fade to black-out*	(Page 48)
Cue 52	**Alan** approaches lighting box, whistling and switches on light *Snap up light on lighting box*	(Page 48)
Cue 53	**Michael:** "... superstitions about *Macbeth*?" *Snap up light on* **Lynne** *in Stage Manager's seat in wings*	(Page 50)
Cue 54	**Alan** moves slide on lighting board *Fade lights gradually*	(Page 51)

Cue 55	**Michael:** "... in front of them." *Fade to black-out except for lighting box*	(Page 51)
Cue 56	**Michael:** "Lightning." *Flash of lightning*	(Page 51)
Cue 57	Wind stops suddenly *Total black-out*	(Page 51)

EFFECTS PLOT

ACT I

MADE AND PRINTED IN GREAT BRITAIN BY
LATIMER TREND & COMPANY LTD PLYMOUTH

MADE IN ENGLAND

COPYRIGHT INFORMATION

(See also page ii)